President Trump

vs

the

Globalists

Paul Colangelo

ISBN (Print): 978-1-09832-455-1
ISBN (eBook): 978-1-09832-456-8

Contents

Introduction

If you are a never Trump person or a fan of President Trump, this book will shed light on both of those positions. Never before has a sitting president been the recipient of overwhelming negative bias by the mainstream media. By most accounts 85 to 93% of the mainstream media coverage regarding President Trump is negative. We've heard it all, he's a racist, misogynistic, he's destroying NATO, he's a climate change denier, he'll get us in a war with North Korea, he dropped the corporate tax rate to give his rich friends a tax break, his tariffs are hurting our economy…and on and on. His record as President states otherwise. When is the last time the main stream media reported on the fact that unemployment is at a 50 year low. Unemployment is at a historic low for both African Americans and Hispanics. Wages are rising. The stock market breaks record after record. That means Americans whose retirement is in the form of 401k's are doing quite well. So why does the mainstream media constantly attack him? Why do you never hear these facts in the main stream media? Is it possible that the mainstream media is controlled by powerful forces that want to weaken America? If so, why? Who are these people and organizations? What is their ultimate goal? Let's get right to it because time is the one thing we are all running out of…on this planet. A prescient quote to keep in mind. "The world is governed by very different personages from what is imagined by those who are not behind the scenes." Benjamin Disraeli, Prime Minister of England from 1874 to 1880.

Chapter One

Council on Foreign
Relations and the Media

"It's good to have an outpost of the council down the street from the State Department. This way I won't have far to go to be told what we should be doing and how we should be thinking about the future." Secretary of State Hillary Clinton speaking at the Council on Foreign Relations new headquarters in Washington D. C. She goes on to say she has been often to the mothership in New York.

If you've heard of the Council on Foreign Relations congratulations. If you have not you are like the vast majority of Americans. From now on we shall refer to it as the CFR. This body of women and men is the most powerful organization in the U. S. Its members have dominated every president's cabinet since FDR, regardless of whether the President in office was Republican or Democrat. What about the presidents themselves? Gary Allen in his bestselling book of 44 years ago, The Rockefeller File, puts it something like this. In 1952 and 1956 you had CFR member Adlai Stevenson running against CFR member Eisenhower. In 1960 it was CFR member Nixon against CFR member Kennedy. In 1964 the conservative arm of the GOP stunned the establishment by nominating its candidate over Nelson Rockefeller. After that the CFR's media wing swung into high gear and began portraying Goldwater as a dangerous radical who would drop an A bomb on Hanoi, abolish social security and in general be a reincarnation of fascist general Mussolini. Basically a similar narrative they used and continue using against President Trump. LBJ won the largest share of the popular vote of any candidate since the largely uncontested election of 1820; the power of the media. In 1968 it was CFR member Nixon against CFR member Humphrey. In 1972 it was Nixon again, this time running against CFR member Mc Govern. After Nixon resigned because of Watergate CFR member Nelson Rockefeller became the unelected Vice President of the United States with CFR member Gerald Ford as The President. I'll pick up here as that book was written in 1976. Then came CFR member Carter, Reagan and George H. W. Bush. You then had CFR member Bill Clinton in the white house after his defeat of Bush. Then it was time for George's son George W. Bush, CFR family member to be president. George W. first ran against CFR member Al Gore, then in 2004 he defeated CFR member John Kerry. After Bush's two terms you had CFR member John McCain against CFR approved Barack Obama. It was McCain who cast the deciding vote against Republican Party lines in favor of the train wreck called Obamacare which sent deductibles skyrocketing. Then it was CFR approved Mitt Romney's turn to take a whack at it against Obama. Mitt Romney while running against Obama was spoken of glowingly by the CFR magazine Foreign Affairs and his presumptive cabinet was to be all CFR members. He has denied being a CFR member. Mitt Romney was the lone Republican to vote for President Trump's impeachment. After that we had CFR family member Hillary Clinton run against outsider Donald Trump. We then had something extraordinary happen. An outsider, a man not approved by the powers that be became president, beating mass media sweetheart Hillary Clinton. His name is President Donald Trump. He's been driving the Globalists nuts ever since. This is why the Globalist controlled media is constantly attacking him. He is undoing decades of their work. I believe that the book and documentary, Clinton Cash, that was easily pulled up by millions of people on their smart phones had an impact on the 2016 election. So you see, the powers that be have owned all the horses in the presidential race since the 1940's with the exception of Goldwater and President Trump. The Globalists did not care if a Republican or a Democrat won. Why would they? They controlled both candidates. Americans have had an illusion of choice. Does it surprise anyone that Hillary could not believe she lost? The fix was in. She still can't believe it. So not only did Hillary have the CFR behind her, she had ABC, CBS, NBC, CNN and of course MSNBC. She also had The New York Times, The Washington Post, Time, Newsweek and many other publications on her side alone. Please know that major articles printed by the New York Times are picked up by most major papers in every state in The United States. So control of the New York Times is paramount. I cringe listening to ABC CFR member George Stephanopoulos breathlessly lead the attack on President Trump every morning on America's favorite morning show, Good Morning America. He also has his own program on ABC's Sunday morning show, This Week with George Stephanopoulos.

George was the senior advisor to Bill Clinton from June 1993 to December 1996. George is also a Bilderberger. The Bilderbergers comprise 120 of the most powerful people in the world. Only the inner circle of the CFR attend their meetings, as well as the Inner circle of the CFR's European counterpart organizations. We'll get to The Bilderbergers a bit later. George is an extremely bright man. It is no accident that he shepherds the information people receive every morning on GMA. What you hear on the news is too important to be left to just anyone. When George is done attacking President Trump, we then typically her from ABC chief White House correspondent, CFR member Johnathan Karl, as he continues the indoctrination. Don't be fooled, it is indoctrination. Repetition is the mother of learning. I'm not saying that every newscaster is a CFR member. Of course not. Most people on your local news simply read what's in front of them. Any twist on the facts is done before it gets to them. The real power is with people like George who twists words to satisfy the Globalist agenda. Do you ever notice how George asks a question and then if the answer is not going the way he wants he rudely interrupts the person speaking and asks another pointed, rhetorical question? He does not ask these questions to hear the other person's truth or even opinion. He frames these questions in a way to make a point. He is a clever man. I can't tell you how many people I've spoken to over the past 3 years about President Trump. When I ask them why they feel the way they do they can't substantiate their beliefs. It's been drilled into their head…Trump bad. What's really sad is innocent young people believe what they hear on the news as gospel. Do you Like Diane Sawyer, how about CBS's and CNN's Katie Couric? They are both members of the CFR. Judy Woodruff of both NBC and PBS, moderator of presidential debates, and well known for interviewing presidents, is a CFR member. Prescott Bush was a U.S. Senator from Connecticut from 1952 to 1963, prior to that he was a partner of A. Harriman & C0, a powerful investment bank. He was also a founder and director of Union Bank. Books have been written about the two banks business dealings with Nazi Germany. He was also the father of George H. W. Bush and grandfather to George W. Bush. He was on the board of directors for CBS. His great granddaughter George W.'s daughter Jenna, miraculously got an anchor spot on NBC's Today, with Hoda &Jenna. All that with no previous experience in the field. What we hear is too important to be left to chance. The mass media, bankers and politicians have always had a sordid relationship. Does anyone think it odd that we had two presidents from the same family a mere 8 years apart? How about Bill for 8 and then nearly Hillary 8 years later. Are these people so extraordinary? Bill's history says no. "I did not have sexual relations with that women, Monica Lewinsky." How about Hillary being asked before the senate if she wiped her server? Her response, "you mean like with a cloth." Hillary is an extremely intelligent woman. When she made that statement she was lying. "You mean like with a cloth" really? If you've heard George W. speak you're pretty certain he's not extraordinary. Because of the Globalist Media's constant barrage we elect people that don't have the best intentions for our country or people in mind. Let's go back in time to the origins of the CFR so that we can better understand our present.

The CFR was started in 1921. The land was donated by the Rockefeller family as was the building. The original headquarters is in Manhattan Island. As stated above they now have a second location in D. C. to be closer to the action. The membership roster consists of approximately 5,000 women and men. They are heads of multi-national corporations including bankers, academics, media moguls, heads of prestigious universities, professors, generals, admirals and politicians. The CFR was the recipient of massive funding in the 1930's from the Rockefeller Foundation,

The Carnegie Foundation and the Ford Foundation. The Rockefeller money continues to flow into the CFR to this day. If you're paying for it you may as well run it. That is exactly what David Rockefeller did for most of his life. Until his death at 101 in 2017, he was still Chairman Emeritus. His nephew John D. Rockefeller IV is a member as well...Nothing changes. His nephew, John D. Rockefeller IV was also both a U. S. Senator from West Virginia as well as governor of West Virginia. David Rockefeller was the Grandson of John D. Rockefeller (1839-1937). According to Forbes, John D. was worth $409 billion dollars in 1913 money adjusted for inflation. In his day he was considered the richest man in the world. He lived and amassed more wealth for an additional 24 years. He had one son, John D. Rockefeller Jr. David Rockefeller was one of Jr's 5 sons. He was born 1915 and died in 2017, just shy of his 102 birthday. I mention his long life to illustrate how much time he had for his nefarious endeavors. During his long life he was responsible for creating the Tri-lateral Commission. The TLC was created to foster closer cooperation between Japan, Western Europe and the U. S. Most Americans have not heard of this powerful organization as well. It's aims are the same as the CFR's but is inclusive of other nations leaders. Other founding members of the TLC included Alan Greenspan and Paul Volcker. They both became heads of the Federal Reserve of the United States. David Rockefeller and his family's money were also instrumental in creating and or financing The Brookings Institute and many more "Think Tanks." He was also instrumental in creating the disaster called NAFTA. We'll get to that train wreck later. Though these organizations call themselves "Think Tanks," history has shown us they do far more than just think. Incidentally the Rockefeller family also donated the land in lower Manhattan for the United Nations. I'm sure most Americans think the Rockefeller wealth, power and influence are a thing of the past. That is extremely unenlightened thinking. The zeal and ruthlessness that patriarch John D. acquired his fortune with makes it highly doubtful he and his progeny let the sands of time erode it. In his day he was known as John D. Reckafella. He trained his only son John D. Rockefeller Jr. the same way. In business he was absolutely ruthless. At one point in time his company, Standard Oil, refined 90% of the oil in the world. Not 90% of the oil in the United States…90% of the oil in the world! The famous monopoly busting attributed to Teddy Roosevelt was largely against him, (Teddy was a cousin of FDR and was not the trustbuster we think, he was part of the Eastern Establishment) it was not successful nor was it planned to be, it did make unenlightened voters happy. The cartoons at the time showed Teddy with a hammer breaking up the trusts. John D. was prepared, ahead of time. He simply broke his oil company (Standard Oil) into many different companies, renamed them and remained in control. This is where having trusts and foundations comes in handy. With an army of the best CPA's, tax attorneys and investment strategists in the country the money and power only grew. The family controls Exon/Mobile, which has revenue coming literally from all over the Earth. You may have heard on CBS that the Rockefeller Family Trust sold their interests in the oil business. The family claiming that in good conscience they could not be involved in manmade climate change due to the burning of fossil fuels. The Rockefeller Family Trust did liquidate their holdings in Exxon/Mobile. Before liquidation they used the funds derived from Exxon/Mobile for philanthropic misdeeds. Gary Allen in his book The Rockefeller File called it the art of scientific giving. The more you give to an organization the more power you have over that organization. Though one trust out of hundreds got out of oil I assure the Rockefellers retained control. They control many other oil companies through a web of trusts and foundations as well. The Rockefeller Trust Company manages 100's of trusts for the family.[1] They are in strong

---

1   managing the family wealth, 1992 New York Times article Rockefeller Family Tries to keep a Vast Fortune from Dissipating.

positions of control in most top 100 companies in the U. S. They are strong in the insurance industry. Some of the trusts and foundations they control bare their name, most do not. When you see a new Chase bank go up, that is a Rockefeller bank in partnership with the Morgan banking family. The full name of the bank is J. P. Morgan Chase. The Morgan family was so powerful that when J. P. Morgan died the stock market did not open until 12:00. That is the only time in history something like that has happened. J. P. Morgan literally bailed out the U. S. government in the panic of 1893.[2] It is the Morgan family that controls your electricity through Edison whom J.P. financed, your nuclear power through the building and construction of the power plants themselves. The power plants are products of GE, yea, they make washers and dryers too. J. P. Morgan/Chase is the most powerful bank in the world. Laurence Rockefeller, David's Older Brother, (1910 – 2004), was an early pioneer in venture capital. He and his four brothers along with their sister Babs created Venrock Associates in 1946. Through this company they provided early capital to both Intel and Apple along with capital for other startups in instrumentation, high temperature physics, nuclear power, health care, aerospace, insurance companies biotech and of course pharmaceuticals.[3] Venrock has invested on the bottom floor of over 270 Companies.[4] Venrock is very big in biotech, for a list of some of the companies they funded see this link: https://www.venrock.com/portfolio/. Think of it in these terms as far as venture capitalism is concerned. You've got billions of dollars at your disposal. You've have ten very sharp men or women in front of your trusted advisor from the computer industry or any other field. Your advisor is an expert in the field of the hopeful startup he will be interviewing. You have experts in many fields working for you. The startup hopeful is interviewed by your man and approved or declined. You finance only the best of the best. Some fail, others become Apple, Intel or something else. Congratulations, you've just expanded the family wealth. You are doing this in a plethora of fields and you've been doing it for 70 years. On top of all that the Morgan/Rockefeller cartel was instrumental in the formation of the United States Federal Reserve. A huge source of revenue. We'll get to the creation of the Fed later. Alright, you get it. They haven't gone away. Their wealth has grown. So what comes after money?

2   *JP Morgan.com.*

3   *Forbes, https://www.google.com/sites/keryyadolan/2013/05/09how-venrock-is-reinventing-itself/ amp/.*

4   *Californiaeconomy.org, https://californiaeconomy.org/content/venrock-associates.*

Power. "We shall have one world government whether we like it or not, the only question is will it be achieved by conquest or consent." James Paul Warburg in his 1950 appearance in front of the U.S. Senate committee on foreign relations, not to be confused with the CFR. James Warburg was the son of Paul Warburg and a CFR member. Paul Warburg was one of the 5 shadow figures that created the Federal Reserve, he was also a founder of the CFR. Nelson Aldrich, the Powerful U.S. Senator from R.I. and head of the Senate Finance Committee was a member of the 5 as well. He was the maternal grandfather of the five Rockefeller brothers.

The Rockefeller family recognized 100 years ago that conquering minds was paramount to their final objective. They have been insidiously wrapping their tentacles around the U. S. educational system. Here is an excerpt from The Rockefeller File by Gary Allen. Research and experimental stations were established at selected Universities, notably Columbia, Stanford and Chicago. Here some of the worst mischief in recent education was born. In these Rockefeller and Carnegie established vineyards worked many of the principle characters in the story of the suborning of American Education. Here foundations nurtured some of the most ardent academic advocates of upsetting the American system and supplanting it with a social state.

The Carnegie and Rockefeller Foundations had jumped into the financing of education and the social sciences with both left feet. During the first two thirds of the 20th century they supplied 20% of the total income of colleges and universities. When you control the purse string you control the curriculum and importantly, which text books are being used and by which authors. You will have a say in the appointments of Deans and Presidents of Universities. Bernie Sanders success with his socialist platform can be attributed to the seeds sown by the Rockefellers 100 years ago. Woodrow Wilson was an early example of their infiltration of our educational system. Prior to being President of the United States he was President of Princeton University. You may be thinking that was a long time ago. Here is a list of College Presidents as of 2016, all are CFR members:

Lee C. Bollinger, President of Columbia University

Eduardo J. Padron, President of Miami Dade College

Christina H. Paxson, President of Brown University

Adam Weinberg, President of Denison University

Leo Reif, President of Massachusetts Institute of Technology

David J. Skorton, President of Cornell University

John J. DeGioia, President of Georgetown University

David L. Boren, President of University of Oklahoma

Donna E. Shalala, President of Miami University

Steven Knapp, President of George Washington University

John Edward Sexton, President of New York University

Kerry Murphy Babson, President of Babson College

Michael K. Young, President of University of Washington

David W. Leebron, President of Rice University

Renu Khator, President of University of Houston

Jeffrey I. of Colgate Herbst, President University

Mark B. Rosenberg, President Of Florida International University

Former College Presidents and CFR members

Neil L. Rudenstine, President of Harvard ((1991-2001)

Benno C. Schmidt Jr., President of Yale (1986-1992)

Richard C. Levin, President of Yale (1993-2013)

George E. Rupp, President of Columbia University (1993-2002)

Michael J. Sovern, President of Columbia University (1980-1993)

Vartan Gregorian, President of Brown University (1989-1997)

Ruth J. Simmons, President of Brown University (2001-2012)

Susan Hockfield, President of MIT (2004-2012)

Hanna Holborn Gray, President of University of Chicago (1979-1993)

Nannerl O. Keohane, President of Duke University (1993-2004)

Gerhard Casper, President of Stanford University (1992-2000)

The list of CFR members who are College Deans is interesting for the reason they are Deans of Foreign Service, International Affairs, International Studies, Government, law and the like. I will provide a list consisting of only the most prestige's of Educational establishments as I think the point has been made that our schools have been infiltrated.

Carol J. Lancaster, Dean of Edmound A. Walsh School of Foreign Service at Georgetown University (2009-2016)

Merit E. Janow, Dean of School of International Affairs at Columbia University (2013-2016)

R. Glenn Hubbard, Dean of Columbia Business School (2004-2016)

Jessica P. Einhorn, Dean, Paul Nitze School of Advanced Int'l Studies at Johns Hopkins Univ. (2002-2012)

Anthoney T. Kronman, Dean of Yale Law School (1994-2004)

Graham T. AllisonJr. Dean of Kennedy School of Government at Harvard Univ. (1977-1989)

Albert Carnesale, Dean of Kennedy School of Government at Harvard Univ. (1991-1995)

Joeseph S. Nye Jr., Dean of Kennedy School of Government at Harvard Univ. (1995-2004)

Alfred C. Stepan, Dean of School of International and Public Affairs at Columbia Univ. (1983-1991)

Lisa Anderson, Dean of School of International and Public Affairs at Columbia Univ, (1997-2007)

Anne-Marie Slaughter, Dean of Woodrow Wilson School of Public and Int'l Affairs at Princeton Univ. (2001-2009)

Regarding the art of scientific giving, here is a list of universities The Rockefeller Foundation, (completely separate from the Rockefeller Family Trust or The Rockefeller Brothers Fund) has been supporting for generations. There are 75 in all. This is a partial list:

Harvard Dartmouth Princeton UC Berkeley Stanford Yale MIT Columbus Cornell Brown Tufts University of Pennsylvania Case Western Reserve University London School of Economics and University College London.[5] Chicago University was started in 1889 by John D. Rockefeller money.

It is the Dean and Presidents of universities who determine which professors get hired. These right minded professors then teach other would be professors and high school teachers who then teach your children. This has been going on for one hundred years. I am not saying that all teachers and college professors are part of a conspiracy, that would be idiotic. I am saying they are being taught by some who are. It's crazy that most people can't name the three branches of government, and if you talk to them about checks and balances they think they are getting money. Let's see what congress tried to do about it. When a congressional committee, headed by Carroll Reece of Tennessee, attempted to hold an open hearing into the activities of the foundations they ran into a serious wall of opposition from the "powers that be" in the nation's capital and it had to be disbanded. Four years later the Committee's general counsel, Rene Wormser, wrote an expose on the subject, it was titled, Foundations: Their power and influence. Wormer stated that the facts this committee developed "leads to the conclusion that there was, indeed, something in the nature of an actual conspiracy among certain leading educators in the United States to bring about socialism through the use of our school systems. "A variety of foundations and allied organizations has developed over the years to exercise a high degree of control over education. Part of this complex, and ultimately responsible for it, are the Rockefeller and Carnegie groups of foundations."

"The first step in liquidating a people is to erase its memory. Destroy its books, its culture, its history. Then have somebody write new books, manufacture a new culture, invent a new history. Before long the nation will begin to forget what it is and what it was." Milan Kundera.

We see this happening before our eyes with the tearing down of monuments all over the country. With history books being rewritten. The Soviets used to have a saying, "We are the only nation unsure of its history." This has been happening to America for decades. It is rapidly accelerating. ANTIFA

---

5   Robert Shaplen, Toward the Well-Being of Mankind: Fifty Years of the Rockefeller Foundation, New York: Doubleday &n Company, Inc 1964 {passim}.

has just been designated a terrorist organization by President Trump. They are funded by CFR Billionaire George Soros. This is the organization that nearly killed an Asian journalist because he was at one of their peaceful protests. There was no mention of this on the main stream media. They also don't mention the fact that colleges and universities were barring people like Ben Shapiro from speaking on campuses. His constitutional views were deemed by many universities as being divisive and potentially hurtful. Ya gotta be kidding me.

If you wonder why Sanders is doing so well I hope this sheds light upon why. A couple of things. The Carnegie Foundation came under Rockefeller control 60 years ago. When you see anything about the Carnegie foundation, know that it is an arm of the Rockefeller Empire. Secondly, why would people that made themselves billionaires (by now you can be sure that the Rockefeller family is worth trillions) under capitalism want socialism? The socialism is for you and me, not them. Socialism is an economic assassin. Socialism is yet another mechanism for control and globalization.

"We are grateful to the Washington Post, The New Your Times, Time magazine and many other great publications whose directors have attended our meetings and respected their promises of discretion for almost 40 years. It would have been impossible for us to develop our plans for the future had we been subjected to the lights of publicity during those years. But, the world is more sophisticated and prepared to march towards a world government. The supranational sovereignty of an intellectual elite is surely preferable to the national auto-determination practiced in the last century." David Rockefeller.

"For more than a century ideological extremists at either end of the political spectrum have seized upon well publicized incidents such as my encounter with Castro to attack the Rockefeller family for the inordinate influence they claim we have over American political and economic institutions. Some even believe we are part of a secret Cabal working against the best interests of the United States, characterizing my family and me as internationalists and of conspiring with others around the world to build a more integrated global political and economic structure...one world if you will. "If that's the charge I stand guilty and proud of it." David Rockefeller. Why would a man who had worked in the shadows and shunned publicity make such a statement? Only he knows. I have a hypotheses. I believe it was ego and hubris. I think he may have thought, I'm the scion of one of the two most powerful families in the world, I'm done hiding. Why hide anymore, we got this. And then came Trump.

I seriously doubt all 5,000 members of the CFR are power mad Globalists. There have been some good men that were invited in and stayed to see what was going on. Call it knowing Thy enemy. I get that rag Time Magazine for that very purpose, (Time magazine by the way has a worldwide circulation of 100 million, It's new owner Marc Benioff, is of course, a CFR member as was the founder Henry Luce). Some CFR members that write regularly for Time include: Ian Bremmer and Fareed Zakaria, who writes for Newsweek, the Washington post and has his own show on CNN as well. Also General David H. Petraeus, former commander of U. S. military operation in Iraq. There are some good guys, Newt Gingrich and Admiral Chester Ward to name a few. Admiral Ward spoke out against them over 45 years ago. Admiral Chester Ward was one that knew what the CFR's true aim was. He finally quit in disgust. He then wrote a book called Kissinger on the Couch. Here is a quote from that book. "[The CFR has a goal] submergence of U. S. sovereignty and national independence into an all-powerful one world government…this lust to surrender sovereignty and independence of the United States is pervasive throughout most of its membership… in the entire CFR lexicon there is no term of revulsion carrying a meaning so deep as "America First." America first sounds familiar, maybe President Trump read that book? It stands to reason that a great many CFR members do not know what the true goals of the top echelon are. Just as the factory worker of 50 years ago didn't know his factory and his job were to be shipped off to a third world country where the corporate taxes were much lower by Globalist design. So how's the CFR work? Picture circles inside of circles. The people in the outer circle will never know the true aims of the CFR. They will not be privy to those types of meetings. They are very necessary as they can honestly and believably say, "I've been a CFR member for 20 years and I've never heard anything like that from another member." The people in the next smaller circle are perhaps being watched and evaluated for more serious tasks in the future. They must earn trust which is not easily given. They are not sure what the true aims of the CFR are. A smaller circle has an idea but perhaps choose not to admit in their inner soul what they suspect is going on. They want the wealth and connections. A third smaller group knows what's happening and does not care for reasons of wealth and economic connections. A fourth group knows what's happening and erroneously believe a one world government would end war, poverty, hunger, and all manner of human ills. These are the truly misinformed. A look back at wars, economic upheavals causing hunger, disease, ethnic cleansing and more would show this group that the very people they wish to trust with the world, are the ones who caused many of its current ills. The next smaller group embraces what's happening. They know the power of the people in the inner circle. They know their power is nearly complete. They think why fight the overwhelming tide. They know that President Trump is not one of them. They know in 4 or 8 years when he is gone it will be back to business as usual. Lastly, there are the people in the smallest circle. They think they are the true rulers of this world. If you are a Christian and believe in dispensational premillennialism (the rapture and the following 7 year tribulation period) this coming global government makes a great deal of sense to you. How else are you going to get all people great and small to take the mark? If you are not a Christian this lust for power is no less real. So in case you think I'm nuts, we have a former first lady, U. S. Senator and Secretary of State stating where the true power is and kowtowing to them. We have the grandson of one of the founders of The Federal Reserve telling us we shall have a one world Government. We the have the last surviving grandson of John D. Rockefeller telling us the same thing. On top of that we have a U. S. Admiral saying the same thing 40 plus years ago and writing a book about it. The European Union is a huge step toward world government 50 years in the making. The EU has no borders (just on maps), a united military, one currency and unelected officials in Belgium running it all. The Pope wanted to know why in the EU's constitution there is no mention of God. If you're interested in worshipping your God the way you see fit, a world government is not going to be good for you. Let me go just a bit further for any remaining doubters.

Carroll Quigley was a professor of economics at Georgetown University. Georgetown is Bill Clinton's alma mater. Bill also attended the University of Oxford as a Rhodes Scholar. Cecil Rhodes, for whom the term Rhodes Scholar comes, was an early Globalist. His wealth came from the diamond mines of Southern Africa. You may remember a nation called Rhodesia. It was named after Cecil Rhodes. He was one of the originators of the round table groups in Europe of which the CFR and the Trilateral Commission are the American arm. Bill Clinton got his globalist training first with Carroll Quigley and then at Oxford. Some notable Rhodes scholars in today's world are: Cory Booker, United States Senator from New Jersey and

Democratic Presidential hopeful. Susan Rice, U. S. Ambassador to the U. N. and close Obama advisor. Rachel Maddow, MSNBC anchor and top Trump Derangement Syndrome sufferer. Dean Rusk, former secretary of State for both Kennedy and Johnson and lastly for this list, George Stephanopoulos.

The heads of state that were awarded Rhodes Scholarships are typically heads of former British Colonies with the exception of Clinton, they include: Wasim Sajjad (Pakistan), Dan Mintoff (Malta), John Turner (Canada), Norman Manley (Jamaica), and Bob Hawk, Tony Abbott and Malcom Turnbull, all from Australia.

There are many more well-known individuals in the fields of education, philosophy, biotech and other fields but I believe that point has been made.

Back to Carroll. In his 1,300 plus page book Tragedy and Hope, he states that he had studied the above groups for twenty years. He then goes on to say that he was made privy to their documents for two years. His only argument with the globalist groups was that they wanted to remain hidden. Towards the end of his life he realized the group's intent was not good but evil. Carroll was more than just a professor of Clintons, he was his globalist mentor. In Bill Clinton's inaugural address he thanked Professor Quigley for his guidance and mentorship. Here is a quote from Dr. Quigley's book. "The powers of financial capitalism had another far-reaching aim, nothing less than to create a world system of financial control in private hands able to dominate the political system of each country and the economy of the world as a whole," he explained on page

324 of his book. "This system was to be controlled in a feudalistic fashion by the central banks of the world acting in concert, by secret agreement arrived at in frequent meetings and conferences. The apex of the system was to be the Bank of International Settlements (BIS) in Basil, Switzerland, a private bank owned and controlled by the world's central banks which were themselves private corporations." More on the United States Central Bank in the next chapter.

So, we have a U.S. president admitting that he was mentored by a Globalist who was privy to the documents of the Globalists for two years. We've got a nearly 100 year old organization whose top pinnacle membership/leadership includes super rich families that have had billions of dollars in their families for over 100 years. We know that they were/are so close to realizing their goals that they just had to tell the world. We also know that they like to work in the shadows. When you have to hide what you're doing that means you are probably not doing good for others. It is disheartening to me that some individuals' think a global government would be good for mankind. They do not realize the old adage that power corrupts and absolute power corrupts absolutely, is true. It is in our nature as humans. Unfortunately the mass media the Globalists control is expert at creating public opinion. When you hear something over and over you start believing it, especially if you hear it from different TV stations and news publications. Repetition truly is the mother of learning, or brain washing if you like. For those people that may think these families should run this world government (don't get it twisted, they would be in control) Here are a few events in history that occurred for different reasons than those not themselves behind the scenes imagine. They are not what I would call good for mankind. Two of the following events (False Flags) occurred before the formation of the CFR. The power and people behind the events were the creators of the CFR. Now their sons and grandsons have assumed the mantle of power.

For we wrestle not against flesh and blood, but against principalities, against powers, against the rulers of darkness of this world, against spiritual wickedness in high places. Ephesians 6:12

What if I told you that the Battleship Maine was blown up not by the Spanish, but to get us into The Spanish American War. That the Germans told the United States that they were going to torpedo the luxury liner Lusitania which got The United States into WW1. That our government knew the Japanese were going to bomb Pearl Harbor. That we were not allowed to end the war quickly in Viet Nam. Let's stop there because you may be thinking I'm nuts. I am not. I do not believe in little green men, ancient aliens, pyramid power, reptilian hybrids, Anunnaki or any other whack subjects. I am also quit sure that there is not a monster in my closet. I'm speaking of power hungry men who want a world government with themselves in complete control. George H. W. Bush was the first president to use the term "New world Order." When someone exposes this group they are dismissed by the uninformed as a "Conspiracy Theorist." Good people have a problem believing in evil on the scale of these globalists because good people are not evil. Even Christians have a hard time with it, and they know Satan is hard at work. At the same time people believe organized crime exists. They think what it does is evil. They believe that organized crime kills. Organized crime exists all over the world. Organized Crime kills for control of the dockyard, aspects of construction, trash routes, drugs, protection money, cybercrime, slavery and a whole lot more. We have serial killers, child rapists and the Catholic Church turning a blind eye for generations as to what their priests were doing, you may have seen the Hollywood movie Spotlight? It's a movie about the Catholic Church turning a blind eye to what its priests have been doing to children for decades. The Globalists kill for control of Countries. They kill millions. Let's keep in mind that J. Edgar Hoover, the top man in the FBI denied the existence of the Mafia as late as the 60's. The mafia started in Sicily 1,000 years ago. It arrived on our shores not in 1900's New York but in the late 1800's in Louisiana. Hoover was the director of the FBI for 37 years, from 1935 to 1977. Yet he was in the dark much of that time regarding the Mafia, just as Americans are in the dark now about Globalists. Would you call serial killers evil? How about suicide bombers? If you're really having a problem with the concept of people being evil and wanting to rule the world, here are a few quick examples.

Julius Caesar was in Gaul (modern day France) from 58BC to 51BC. According to Caesars Commentaries, he killed 250,000 men women and children and enslaved 1,000,000 (he got the lion's share of the money for the slaves). Even after all of that, the Gauls rebelled. What did Caesar do with the survivors of the last rebellion? He cut both hands off of 5,000 warriors and sent them all over Gaul as a warning. He then went back to Rome and became Dictator. Being the Dictator of Rome meant you were the most powerful man in the world at that time. Here we have an example of evil and a lust for power. Regarding Caesar's commentaries, He wrote them. When he was marching with his men he was attended by 6 scribes. He would speak to the first scribe and give that scribe time to write down what he had said, then to the next and so on until he was back to the first scribe. He would then pickup right where he left of and go through all 6 again until he was finished with his "news." These commentaries were then sent to the Roman Senate so that he could control public opinion. This was an early example of media control. From 68 to 69 AD the Roman Empire experienced 4 Emperors. The first three did not die of natural causes. Before Caesar we had Alexander the great. An argument could be made that he conquered the Persian Empire because of earlier attacks by the Persians on Grecian colonies in the near east as well as Greece herself. Ok, makes sense. Why then did he keep going though modern day Afghanistan, Pakistan and into India? The reason he had to stop? His men said we have enough gold and silver, we are not fighting anymore. Alexander was power mad (evil). When you conquer because it's there, that in my mind is evil.

How about Genghis Khan, 1162-1227. This psycho nut job killed millions. He conquered everything in his path from China to Russia to the gates of Constantinople and much of the Middle East including modern day Iran and Iraq. When a city resisted he had his men kill everything that moved, everything! I would call him power mad and evil. The Mongols came from the Gobi desert. The Gobi was located in Mongolia between modern day Russia and China. No country attacked the Mongols in the desert. Why would they? There is not a whole lot of "stuff" in the desert. Genghis conquered for conquest sake. He was asked, what is best in life? His answer: Crush your enemy, see him driven before you, and hear the lamentation of the women. Genghis goes in my evil column. History shows us many men of this ilk. I could go on and on. Hitler, Stalin, Pol Pot, Saddam…Mankind does not change. The Romans were having orgies that made anything the naked zonked out Hippies were doing in the 60's look like tea time with Mother Teresa. Opium was known to the Romans as well, and they had string, horn and drum musical instruments, Sex, drugs and rock and roll. Let's have a look at some Globalist handy work and the Mass Medias involvement. This will serve three purposes: it will enlighten us to the methods and lengths evil men will go to, it will convince us that we don't want these people running a one world government, and it will illuminate us to the mass media's culpability. A simple equation to keep in mind along the way: Healthy economy + really big lie + weak, but plausible excuse + someone else to blame = Social Control.[6]

Spanish American War

The Battleship Maine was in Havana Harbor in 1898. Cuba was a Spanish possession, as was Guam, Puerto Rico and the Philippines. The Cubans were attempting a revolution. We sent our navy and marines there to "help" the Cubans. The Spanish did not want a war with the United States they could not win. Our bankers and industrialists wanted to pilfer Cuba of its people and resources. Something had to happen to justify our military

---

6   *Planet earth, the Final Chapter (pg. 220) Hal Lindsey. Published by Western Front LTD., Beverly Hills, CA.*

taking over. During this time, Frederic Remington, the famous artist, was hired by William Randolph Hearst to illustrate the revolution in Cuba. He was quoted as saying, "everything is quite here, there will be no war, I wish to return." Hearst's response was "Please remain, you furnish the pictures and I'll furnish the war".[7] I few months later the ship was blown up from the inside. Maybe a boiler explode, maybe a paid assassin set off dynamite with a long fuse. After the explosion the newspapers under Hearst's control swung into action resulting in indignation from the American people and calls for war. This is an example of the power of the press. President Trump calls it fake news, in that day it was called yellow journalism, so you see the power of the media. After the defeat of Spain the United States now controlled Cuba. We then immediately took control of Guam, Puerto Rico and the Philippines from the Spanish. America was acquiring oversees possessions…there was blood. Cuba's people and natural resources were now ready to be plundered by U. S. industrialists. Almost immediately after the war $5,000,000 was invested in Cuba alone. That's $5,000,000 1898 dollars. The seeds of the Cuban revolution of 1953 under Castro were sown in 1898. More blood.

A quick word on war before we continue. Can anyone remember a war that was not fought for profit? By profit I mean land, commodities or anything else of value. Let's think back, the crusades, nope, those were fought for spoils and absolution. The eldest son of the Baron, Duke or petty Knight got the land and castle if there was one. The younger sons got a Knighthood and a name, they needed to crusade. They had no inheritance. Of course the rallying cry was save the holy land from the infidels. For the people of lowly means there was absolution. If you went out and killed Muslims that were exercising their God given right of freedom of choice regarding religion, the Pope at the time would forgive your sins… Hmm. Wars require an altruistic reason or perceived threat to justify men fighting and dying. History has shown us that the infidels in many cases treated the conquered people of various places in the Levant better than the so called Christians did. I say that as a Christian. It's horrible how much blood has been spilled in the name of God by Godless men.

What about the civil war, surely that was fought to end slavery right? That is what you and I were taught in school. In its day it was called the rich man's

---

7   PBS > crucible > article.

war. It was fought over unfair tariffs levied on the Southern states, money. In the 1860 nearly all federal revenue came from tariffs. There was no income tax and no corporate tax. The Southern states were paying nearly 80% of these tariffs. The South was rural, the North was industrial. The South was importing goods from England cheaper than they could buy them form the North. Thus the tariffs. This was a long time in the making. You could say things started to get heated in 1828 when congress passed a tariff of 62% on nearly all imported goods. The tariffs protected the North from low priced imported goods. It increased the costs of goods to the South. So now the British for example, are selling less goods to the South, thus making it more difficult to buy Southern cotton. By 1833 South Carolina was already talking about leaving the Union because of the 1828 tariff. The South called it the tariff of abominations. Slavery is what we teach are unsuspecting children in school. Very few men fight and die for altruistic purposes, certainly not enough to field armies. Even those extremely few men who may have wanted to fight, were not going to fight and die for strangers at the additional cost of their wife and children dying of starvation while they were away getting shot at. Welfare in this nation did not appear until 1935 under socialist FDR. Let's see what Abraham Lincoln had to say about slavery. In his first inaugural address he stated "I have no purpose, directly or indirectly, to interfere with the institution of slavery in the states where it now exists. I believe I have no lawful right to do so, and I have no inclination to do so."[8] Even during the war he stated. "My paramount object in this struggle is to save the Union, and it is not either to save or destroy slavery. If I could save the Union without freeing any slave I would do it; and if I could do it by freeing all the slaves I would do it; and if I could do it by freeing some and leaving others alone I would do that also."[9] I thought about putting these next few quotes in this book long and hard. It is not my intent to denigrate Lincoln. I am inserting these quotes as further proof to open the readers mind to the concept of what you were taught in school about history and what you hear in the Globalist controlled media is not always the truth (especially on NBC,CBS,ABC,CNN and MSNBC). You will read many shocking things in this book. More from Lincoln. " I am not ,nor ever have been, in favor of bringing about in any way the social and equality of the white and black races, that I am not nor ever have been in favor of

8   Abraham Lincoln: speeches and writings, 1859-1865.

9   *Quoted by Robert L. Polley, ed., Lincoln: His words and His World (Waukesha, Wisconsin: Country Beautiful Foundation,1965),p.54.*

making voters or jurors of Negros, nor of qualifying them to hold office, nor to intermarry with white people, and I will say in addition to this that there is a physical difference between the white and black races which I believe will forever forbid the two races living together on terms of social and political equality".[10] I sighted that source to let the reader know that this isn't some obscure source, It can be found anywhere…except in grade school history books and most college texts. Wars are always fought for profit. The old saying wars are young men dying and old men getting rich is true. The Emancipation Proclamation was not even issued until 1863. The American Civil War started in 1861. Here is what Otto Von Bismarck had to say about it the assassination of Lincoln: "The death of Lincoln was a disaster for Christendom. There was no man to fill his boots and the bankers went anew to grab the riches. "I fear that foreign bankers with their tortuous tricks will entirely control the exuberant riches of America and use it to systematically corrupt civilization." Bismarck was Minister President of Prussia (1862-1890) and Chancellor of the North German Confederation (1867-1871) then the German Empire (1871-1890).

Lusitania/WW1

The Lusitania was a British ocean liner. It was an extremely fast ship. It was sunk by a German U-Boat May 7th 1915 off the coast of Ireland. It was carrying 128 Americans and over 1,000 British subjects, and tons of armaments. This made her a ship of war. The British government knew it was carrying arms. They did not tell their citizens or the American citizens. This false flag event created war fever among Americans. The mass media at the time (newspapers) swung into action. The Germans became blood thirsty Huns, Huns? Most historians would agree that Huns were Asiatic. I don't know any Germans with Asiatic features. Such is the power of the mass media. Prior to that false flag event Americans were staunchly isolationists. In most Americans view at that time, the Europeans were always fighting amongst themselves. The Hundred years War. The Thirty years War. The Napoleonic Wars and as recently as 1870 the Franco Prussian war. Why in the world would hard working Americans want to get involved in a war an ocean away? They wouldn't. Some horrendous event had to inflame the Americans with righteous indignation, and anger.

---

10   *Lincoln-Douglas debates, Wikipedia: http//bit.ly/2hwqEjw .*

The Germans new the Lusitania was carrying tons of war material. They warned Americans not to embark on the ship. They even paid American newspapers to run articles explaining all this. They were never printed in the papers with the exception of one in Iowa…Iowa? The Lusitania was torpedoed and Americans went to war. After great loss of life the war ended and the International bankers made billions. When countries send their young men to war, oil companies, bankers, munitions makers, food suppliers and anyone with the proper connections always win monetarily. When countries go to war they need money that is not in the national budget. They get the money from international bankers. Have you ever wondered how it is that all nations have debt? The debt is owed to international bankers. Europe's central banks are controlled by the Rothschild family and a few more. Our central bank called the Federal Reserve is controlled by the Rockefellers, Morgans and the Rothschilds. We have a chapter on the creation of the United States Federal Reserve in chapter two. This is where the majority of national debt comes from. It's that simple. The rest is subterfuge. When people tell you it's complicated they are usually lying. So Europeans and Americans died…what changed? Certainly no European national boundaries to any extent. The biggest loser was the Ottoman Empire. They were not part of the club at the time so they had to go. We wanted their stuff, oil. The Ottomans controlled the Middle East at the time. What changed as a result of WW1 was American and European national debt, and our tax burden in the form of payments to the Globalists and millions more dead.

Pearl Harbor/WW2

On December 7, 1941 Pearl Harbor was bombed by the Japanese imperial navy. History has taught us that the United States was taken completely by surprise. There are two serious problems with this bit of fiction, radar and American code breakers. Before I go on I want you to know that 40 years ago you were dismissed as a crackpot if you let it be known that you think the U. S. Government knew the Japanese were coming, now historians are having serious debates about it. Many of the historians that argue we didn't know the Japanese were coming are now admitting that yes, we knew they were coming. If you have not heard anything or read anything about this debate that means that you simply haven't heard or read anything about it. That does not make it untrue. Before picking up this book many of you had not heard of the CFR and The Trilateral Commission. The vast majority of historians agree, we had cracked the Japanese code prior to the attack on

Pearl Harbor. On October 9, 1941 we intercepted and decoded a Japanese message telling their American spies to map a grid where our warships were. The message did not say which port. Months before this map was ordered FDR moved our fleet from San Diego Ca. to Pearl. He wanted our fleet closer to the Japanese because they were invading all over the East. So, FDR had the foresight to move the fleet to Hawaii but couldn't figure out that Pearl, with the flower of our fleet there, was the target. It is also interesting to note that that our aircraft carriers were not at Pearl. The war in the pacific, because of its vast size was to be a carrier war. Though the outcome of the war was never in question the Globalists didn't want the Japanese having to big a head start. The second problem, radar. Reliable Radar had been around since the early 1930's. Nikola Tesla Stated the following in 1917, "we may determine the relative position or course of a moving object, such as a vessel at sea, the distance traversed by the same, or its speed". [11] That was in 1917. The British were light years ahead of the rest of the world when it came to this technology. Their survival depended on it. When the Luftwaffe was on it's way to attack the British in WW2 the RAF (Royal Air Force) was already in the air waiting to engage them. Though the United States had radar it was primitive compared to what the British had. The British shared this technology with the U. S. in early 1940, almost two years before Pearl Harbor. They shared this technology as partial payment for the help FDR was giving them with the lend lease act. We were supplying the British with everything but the kitchen sink to help them survive the Nazi on slot. Why didn't we have radar on Guam? It was ours at the time and it is only 1,619 miles from the heart of Japan. We are to believe that a fleet of 6 Aircraft Carriers, 8 cruisers, 30 destroyers,4 subs and 50 other ships attacked Pearl and we didn't know they were coming?

Let me go a little further on the whole we were caught completely by surprise fallacy. In an article in the New American titled Pearl Harbor: Hawaii Was Surprised; FDR was not. There is an article by James Perloff that appeared in December, 2019 of the New American. Here is the link if you'd like to read the article in its entirety:[12] Comprehensive research has shown not only that Washington knew in advance of the attack on Pearl Harbor, but that it deliberately withheld its foreknowledge from our commanders in Hawaii

11   http://www.teslascience.org/pages/tesla.htm#warden.
12   Http//www.thenewamerican.com/culture/history/itm4740-pearl-harbor-hawaii-was-surprised-fdr-was-not.

in the hope that the "surprise" attack would catapult the U. S. into WW2. Much new light has been shed on Pearl Harbor through the recent work of Robert B. Stinnett, a World War 2 navy veteran. Stinnett has obtained numerous relevant documents through the freedom of information act. In Day of Deceit: The Truth about FDR and Pearl Harbor (2000), Stinnett proves beyond doubt that FDR and members of his cabinet were maneuvering the Japanese into war. After meeting with President Roosevelt on October 16th 1941, Secretary of War Henry Stimson wrote in his diary: We face the delicate question of the diplomatic fencing to be done so as to be sure Japan is put into the wrong and makes the first bad move- overt move. Stimson was a Skull and Bones Member, a sister organization to the CFR. Three American Presidents were also members of this extremely secret, extremely exclusive society. A bit more on that later. On November 26th, the U. S. delivered an ultimatum to Japan that demanded, as prerequisites to resumed trade, that Japan withdraw all troops from China and Indochina, and in effect abrogate her Tripartite Treaty with Germany and Italy. On November 25th, the day before the ultimatum was sent to Japan's ambassadors, Stimson wrote in his diary: "The question was how we should maneuver them (the Japanese) into the position of firing the first shot….." The bait offered Japan was our Pacific Fleet. In 1940, Admiral J. O Richardson, the fleet's commander, flew to Washington to protest FDR's decision to permanently base the fleet in Hawaii instead of its normal berthing on the U. S. West Coast. The Admiral had sound reasons: Pearl Harbor was vulnerable to attack, being approachable from any direction it could not be effectively rigged with nets and baffles to defend against torpedo planes, and in Hawaii it would be hard to supply and train crews for his undermanned vessels. Pearl Harbor also lacked adequate fuel supplies and dry docks, and keeping men far from their families would also create moral problems. The argument became heated. Said Richardson: I came away with the impression that, despite his spoken word, that the President was fully determined to put the United States into the war if Great Britain could hold out until he was reelected."

Richardson was quickly relieved of command. Replacing him was Admiral Husband E. Kimmel. Kimmel also informed Roosevelt of Pearl Harbors deficiencies, but accepted placement there, trusting that Washington would notify him of any intelligence pointing to attack. This proved to be a misplaced trust. As Washington watched japan preparing to assault Pearl Harbor, Admiral Kimmel, as well as his Army counterpart in Hawaii, General Walter C. Short, were completely sealed off from the information pipeline. Authors note, when writing about something like our government knowing the attack on Pearl Harbor was coming, I think that most people think that hundreds if not thousands would have had to have been culpable, or in on it. I think these last few paragraphs illustrate that with a few men in the right places much evil can be accomplished. I want to remind the reader that the President of the United States is also the Commander and Chief. Before we go on a quick word on the Delano Family from which FDR descends on his mother's side. Warren Delano Jr. was the maternal grandfather of Franklin Delano Roosevelt. The Delano family Forebears included the pilgrim who chartered the Mayflower. Past President Calvin Coolidge descends from the Delano side. Warren Delano Jr. made his fortune in the Opium trade. Today he would be called a drug dealer. Delano was partners in the Opium trade with William Russell, the founder of Skull and Bones. The Astor Family and the Forbes family also made fortunes in the trade. Warren Delano Jr., in his letters admitted that opium had an "unhappy effect" on its users, but argued that its sale was "fair, honorable, and legitimate," akin to importing wine and spirits to America. Even back then the U. S. government was culpable in the trade. When necessary the trade was assisted by the U. S. government's military humiliating the Chinese government.[13] If you look up the families referred to as Robber Barons in the late 1800's and early 1900', you will find crime. You will also find that many of them are interconnected by marriage. For instance FDR's son married Ethel du Pont heir to the du Pont fortune (sometimes spelled Du Pont), the Du Pont family was known as the merchants of death. They made the majority of the munitions for the Union in the civil war as well as the U. S. in WW1. Now they make chemicals such as Teflon for non-stick pans that kill people. What was their tag line a few years ago? You, me and Du Pont. Makes me wanna toss my cookies.

One of the most important elements in America's foreknowledge of Japan's intentions was our government's success in cracking Japan's secret diplomatic code known as 'Purple. "Tokyo used it to communicate with its embassies and consulates, including those in Washington and Hawaii. The code was so complex that it was enciphered and deciphered by a machine. A talented group of American cryptanalysts broke the code in 1940 and devised a

13   *Five elite Families Who Made Their Fortunes in the Opium Trade. By Phillip Smith, Alternet.org.* *https://www.google.com/amp/s/www.alternet.org/2015/06/5-elite-families-fortunes-opium-trade/amp.*

facsimile of the Japanese machine. These, utilized by the intelligence sections of both the war and navy departments, swiftly revealed Japan's diplomatic messages. The deciphered texts were nicknamed "Magic."

Copies of "magic" were always promptly delivered in locked pouches to President Roosevelt, and the secretaries of State, War, and the navy. Authors note, the preceding three secretary positions are all political appointments. They also went to Army Chief of Staff George Marshall. George Marshall was a CFR member, the Marshall Plan that cost American tax payers billions to rebuild and feed Germany after the war was of course named after him. Marshall then became Secretary of State under Truman. He was also instrumental in the defeat of the nationalists for control of China under Chiang Kai-shek. Due to his backstabbing of Chiang we now have communist China rather than the pro-democracy government of Taiwan, which is where Chiang and his followers had to flee. He did this by brokering a cease fire when Chiang and his followers had the communists on the ropes. Chiang Kai-shek and some historians' later claimed that the cease-fire, under pressure of Marshall, saved the Communists from defeat.[14]

The two Hawaiian commanders were kept completely in the dark by Washington. A request for their own decoding machines was rebuffed on the grounds that diplomatic traffic was of insufficient interest to soldiers. Author again, that's the lamest lie I have ever heard in my life!

On October 9, 1941, the War Department decoded a Tokyo to Honolulu dispatch instructing the Japanese Counsel General to divide Pearl Harbor into five specified areas and to report the exact locations of American ships therein.

There is nothing unusual about spies watching ship movements, but reporting precise whereabouts of ships in docks has only one implication. Charles Willoughby, Douglass MacArthur's chief of intelligence, later wrote that the "reports were on a grid system of the inner harbor with coordinate locations of American Men of War...coordinate grid is the classic method for pinpoint target designation, our battleships had suddenly become

---

14   [Who did Chiang Kai-shek hate most with his withdrawal from Taiwan? Diary says it's not Mao Zedong]. Xin Hua Net. July 31, 2013.

targets." This information was never sent to Kimmel and Short, the Navy and Army Commanders.

Additional intercepts were decoded by Washington, all within one day of their original transmission.

November 5th: Tokyo notifies its Washington Ambassadors that November 25th was the deadline for an agreement with the U. S.

November 11th: They were warned, "The situation is nearing a climax, and the time is getting short.

November16th: The deadline was pushed up to November 29th. "The deadline absolutely cannot be changed" the dispatch said. "after that, things are automatically going to happen." Authors note, in other words the Japanese ships were on their way to bomb Pearl Harbor.

November 29th: (the U. S. ultimatum had now been received): The Japanese Ambassadors were told a rupture in negotiations was "inevitable, "but that Japans leaders "do not wish you to give the impression that negotiations are broken off."

November 30th: Tokyo ordered its Berlin Embassy to inform the Germans that "the breaking out of war may come quicker than anyone dreams."

December 1st and 2nd: The Japanese embassies in non- Axis nations around the world were directed to depose of their secret documents and all but one copy of their codes. (This was for a reason easy to fathom, when war breaks out, the diplomatic offices of a hostile state lose their immunity and are normally over taken. One copy of code was retained so that final instructions could be received, after which the last code copy would be destroyed.) An Additional warning came via the so called "Winds" message. A November 18th intercept indicated that, if a break in U. S. relations were forthcoming, Tokyo would issue a special radio warning. This would not be in Purple code, as it was intended to reach consulates and lessor agencies of Japan not equipped with the code or one of its machines. The message to be repeated three times during the weather report was "Higashi no kaze ame," meaning "East wind, rain." "East wind' signified the United States; "rain" signified diplomatic split, in effect war. This prospective message was deemed so important that U. S. radio monitors were constantly watching for it, and the Navy Department typed it up on special reminder cards. On December 4th, "Higashi no kaze ame" was indeed broadcast and picked up by Washington intelligence.

On three occasions since 1894, Japan had made surprise attacks coinciding with breaks in diplomatic relations. This history was not lost on President Roosevelt. Secretary Stimson, describing FDR's White House conference of November 25th, noted: "The President said the Japanese were notorious for making an attack without warning and stated that we might be attacked, say next Monday, for example." Nor was it lost on Washington's senior military officers, all of them war College graduates.

As Robert Stinnett has revealed, Washington was not only deciphering Japanese diplomatic messages, but naval dispatches as well. The article goes on to state that there was so much secrecy surrounding the naval dispatches that there existence was unknown during any of the ten Pearl Harbor investigations, even the mini probe that congress conducted in 1995. Most of Stinnetts's requests for documents concerning Pearl Harbor have been denied as still classified, even under the freedom of information act.

I am wondering what possible reason there could be for keeping these documents classified? The conclusion I draw is that the "Deep State" as President Trump calls it, is alive and well, as of 2000 anyway when the book was written.

Stinnett's book tells us more, again drawing on the documents he was able to get from the freedom of information act. To insure a successful Japanese attack, one that would enrage America into joining the war, It was vital to keep Kimmel and Short (the two Pearl Harbor Commanders) out of the intelligence loop. However Washington did far more than that to facilitate the Japanese assault.

On November 25th, approximately one hour after the Japanese attack force left port for Hawaii, the U. S. Navy issued an order forbidding U. S. and allied shipping to travel via the North Pacific. All transpacific shipping was rerouted through the South Pacific. This order was even applied to Russian ships docked on the American west coast. The purpose is easy to Fathom. If any commercial ship accidentally stumbled on the Japanese task force, it might alert Pearl Harbor. As Rear Admiral Richard K. Turner, the Navy's War Plans officer in 1941, frankly stated: "We were prepared to divert traffic when we believed war was imminent. "We sent the traffic down the Torres Strait, so that the track of the Japanese force would be clear of any traffic."

The Hawaiian commanders have been censured for failing to detect the approaching Japanese Carriers. What goes unsaid is that Washington denied them the means to do so. An army marching overland toward a target is easily spotted. But Hawaii is in the middle of the ocean. Its approaches are limitless and uninhabited. During the week before December 7th, naval aircraft searched more than 2 million miles of the Pacific, but never saw the Japanese force. This is because Kimmel and Short only had enough planes to survey one third of the 360 degree arc around them, and intelligence had advised them to concentrate on the Southwest. There were not enough trained surveillance pilots as well. Many of the reconnaissance craft were old and suffered from a lack of spare parts. The commanders repeated requests to Washington for additional patrol planes were turned down. Rear Admiral Edward T. Layton, who served at Pearl Harbor, summed it up in his book: And I was There: "There was never any hint in any intelligence received by the local command of any Japanese threat to Hawaii. Our air defenses were stripped on orders from the army chief himself. Of the 12 B-17's on the island, only 6 could be kept in the air by cannibalizing the others for spare parts."

The navy has traditionally followed the rule that, when international relations are critical, the fleet puts to sea. That is exactly what Admiral Kimmel did. Aware the U. S. –Japanese relations were deteriorating, he sent 46 warships safely into the North Pacific in late November 1941- without notifying Washington. He even ordered the fleet to conduct a mock air raid on Pearl Harbor, clairvoyantly selecting the same launch site Yamamoto used two weeks later. When the White House learned of Kimmel's move it countermanded his orders and ordered all ships returned to dock, using the dubious excuse that Kimmel's actions might provoke the Japanese. Washington knew that if the two fleets met at sea, and engaged each other, there might be a question of who fired the first shot.

Kimmel did not give up, however. With the exercise cancelled, his carrier chief, Vice Admiral William "Bull" Halsey, issued plans for a 25 ship task force to guard against an "enemy air and submarine attack" on Pearl

Harbor. The plan never went into effect. On November 26th, Admiral Stark, Washington Chief of Naval Operations, ordered Halsey to use his carriers to transport fighter planes to Wake and Midway Islands-further depleting Pearl's air defenses.

It was clear of course, that once disaster struck Pearl Harbor, there would be demands for accountability. Washington seemed to artfully take this into account by sending an ambiguous "war warning" to Kimmel, and a similar one to Short, on November 27th. This has been used for years by Washington apologists to allege that the commanders should have been ready for the Japanese. Indeed, the message began conspicuously: "This dispatch is to be considered a war warning." But it went on to state: "The number and equipment of Japanese troops and the organizations of naval task forces indicates an amphibious expedition against the Philippines, Thai or Kra Peninsula, or possibly Borneo." None of these areas was closer than 5,000 miles from Hawaii! NO threat to Pearl was hinted at. It ended with the words: "Continental districts, Guam, Samoa take measures against sabotage." The message further stated that "measures should be carried out so as not to alarm the population." Both commanders reported the actions taken to Washington. Short followed through with sabotage precautions, bunching his planes together (which hinders saboteurs but makes ideal targets for bombers), and Kimmel stepped up air surveillance and sub searches. If their responses to the "war warning" was insufficient, Washington said nothing. The next day, a follow up message from Marshal's adjutant general to Short warned only: "Initiate forthwith all additional measures necessary to provide for protection of your establishments, property, and equipment against sabotage, protection of your personal against subversives propaganda and protection of all activities against espionage." Author's note: Regarding the last paragraph, what a bunch of nonsense.

Thus things stood as Japan prepared to strike. Using the Purple code, Tokyo sent a formal statement to its Washington ambassadors. It was to be conveyed to the American Secretary of State on Sunday, December 7th. The statement terminated relations and was tantamount to a declaration of war. On December,6th, in Washington, the War and Navy departments had already decrypted the first 13 parts of this 14 part message. Although the final passage officially severing ties had not yet cone through, the fiery wording made its meaning obvious. Later that day, when Lieutenant Lester

Schulz delivered to President Roosevelt his copy of the intercept, Schulz heard FDR say to his advisor, Harry Hopkins, "This means War."

During subsequent Pearl Harbor investigations, both General Marshall, Army Chief of Staff, and Admiral Stark, Chief of Navy Operations, denied any recollection of where they had been on the evening of December 6th- despite Marshall's reputation for having a photographic memory. But James G. Stahlman, a close friend of Navy Secretary Frank Knox, said Knox told him FDR convened a high level meeting at the White House that evening. Marshall, Knox and War Secretary Stimson attended. Indeed, with the nation on wars threshold, such a conference only made sense. That same evening, the Navy Department received a request from Stimson for a list of the whereabouts of all ships in the Pacific. On the morning of December 7th, the final portion of Japan's lengthy message to the U. S. Government was decoded. Tokyo added to special directives to its ambassadors. The first directive, which the message called "very important," was to deliver the statement at 1 p.m. The second directive ordered that the last copy of code, and the machine that went with it, be destroyed. The gravity of this was immediately recognized in the Navy Department. Japan had a long history of synchronizing attacks with breaks in relations; Sunday was an abnormal day to deliver diplomatic messages-but the best for trying to catch U. S. forces at low vigilance; and on p.m. in Washington was shortly after dawn in Hawaii. Admiral Stark arrived at hi office at 9:25a.m. He was shown the message and the important delivery time. One junior officer pointed out the possibility of an attack on Hawaii: another urged that Kimmel be notified. But Stark refused; he did nothing all morning. Years later, he told the press that his conscious was clear concerning Pearl Harbor because all his actions had been dictated by a "higher authority." As Chief of naval Operations, Stark had only one higher authority: Roosevelt. In the War Department, where the 14 part statement had been decoded, Colonel Rufus Bratton, head of the Army's Far Eastern Section, discerned the messages' significance. But the chief of intelligence told him nothing could be done until Marshall arrived. Bratton tried reaching Marshall at home, but was repeatedly told the general was out horseback riding. The horseback ride turned out to be a long one. When Bratton finally reached Marshall by phone and told him of the emergency, Marshall said he would come to the War Department. Marshall took 75 minutes to make the ten minute drive. He didn't come to his office until 11:25 a.m. - an extremely late hour with the nation on the brink of war. He perused the Japanese message and was shown the delivery time. Every officer in Marshall's office agreed these indicated an attack in the Pacific at about 1 p. m. EST. The general finally agreed that Hawaii should be alerted, but time was running out.

Marshall had only to pick up his desk phone to reach Pearl Harbor on the transpacific line. Doing so would not have averted the attack, but at least our men would have had time to man their battle stations. Instead, the general wrote a dispatch. After it was encoded it went to the Washington office of Western Union. From there it was relayed to San Francisco. From San Francisco it was transmitted via RCA commercial radio to Honolulu. General Short received it 6 hours after the attack. Two hours later it reached Kimmel. One can imagine their exasperation on reading it. Despite all the evidence accrued by Magic and other sources during the previous months, Marshall had never warned Hawaii. To historians-ignorant of that classified evidence- it would appear the general had tried to save Pearl Harbor, "but alas, too late." Similarly, FDR sent a last minute plea for peace to Emperor Hirohito. Although written a week earlier, he did not send it until the evening of December 6th. It was to be delivered by Ambassador Grew, who would be unable to receive an audience with the Emperor until December 8th. Thus the message could not conceivably forestalled the attack-but posterity would think that FDR, too, had made "a valiant, last effort."

The Roberts Commission, assigned to investigate the Japanese attack, consisted of personnel cronies of Roosevelt and Marshall. The Commission fully absolved Washington and declared that America was caught off guard due to "dereliction of duty" by Kimmel and Short. The wrath of America for these two was exceeded only by its wrath for Tokyo. To this day many believe it was negligence by the Hawaii commanders that made the Pearl Harbor disaster possible.

When I was in school the history books said that FDR was doing anything he could to get the U.S. into the war. It is a historical fact that in the election of 1940 FDR ran on a strong isolationist platform. He would "keep our boys out of war". That part was not in the history books in high school. A politician saying one thing to get into office and doing another, I'm shocked! Somewhat like George H. W. Bush's "No new taxes." He then passed one of the biggest tax increases in U. S. History. How about his son's nonexistent weapons of mass destruction that were never found yet propelled the United States into war in Iraq. Or Obama saying if you like your Dr. you can keep him. FDR was the first president with a cabinet full of CFR members. His problem was Americans simply did not want to get into another European conflict. As far as the Japanese in the Far East, that was worlds away from America and not our problem. Remember the world was a different place in 1941. You could not hit your remote control and listen to an English speaking reporter in China tell you all about the war in China with video footage. You had to rely on the newspaper and the radio. This is why FDR's fireside chats regarding the evil Japanese were so powerful. If the President is saying it, it must be true. Think of the power the owners of large papers, magazines and radio stations wielded. Henry Luce, April 3, 1898- February 28th 1967 was called the most influential private citizen of his day. He owned Time, Life, Fortune, Sports Illustrated and numerous radio stations. He was a well-known internationalist and CFR member. So Luce and FDR are warming up the public with anti-Japanese rhetoric. Unfortunately print is sacred. When most people read something they think it is true. John Toland, in his book, Infamy, Pearl Harbor and its Aftermath, states that FDR, William Knox and John Simpson new the attack was coming because of our British supplied technologically advanced radar. So now we have two books written twenty years apart. Both saying we had cracked the Japanese code and both saying we had technologically advanced radar supplied by the British. Knox was a CFR member and director of Westinghouse, a Morgan Company. He was instrumental in supplying the Soviets with mobile power plants in WW2. Simpson was also a CFR member. He was a director of Bechtel, a construction company that built refineries and pipelines for Standard oil in California in 1925 and beyond. He was also a director of Schroder's, an international bank affiliated with the Warburg banking family. Paul Warburg was a Rothschild agent and one of the men that helped create the United States Federal Reserve. We can't leave out Rockefeller man John J. McCloy (March 1895 to March 1989), when speaking of WW2 and beyond. He was a Harvard graduate and attorney. Prior to the war he taught the Rockefeller boys how to sail. To say he had close ties with the Rockefeller family is an understatement. During the war he was the Assistant Secretary of war. You need insiders in positions like Assistant Secretary of War to help keep a lid on the fact that the Japanese are coming to bomb Pearl. During the war he was most directly responsible for putting patriotic U. S. citizens of Japanese descent in internment camps. From 1947 till 1949 he was the U. S. High Commissioner of occupied Germany. During the Nuremberg trails he gave a full pardon to Friedrick Flick and Alfried Krupp. If you've not heard of the Krupp family they were German munitions makers with a 100 plus year history of creating bigger and better stuff to kill people. McCloy then granted them full restitution of all their property. It's important that someone make the bullets for the next war. Germany is regularly one of the top five munitions makers in the world. Here's a quote from Nuremberg Judge William J. Wilkins, "Imagine my surprise one day in January 1951 to read in the newspaper that High Commissioner John J. McCloy had restored all of the Krupp properties that had been confiscated." From 1946 to 1949 and again from 1953 to 1960 he was Chairman of Chase Manhattan Bank. From 1954 to 1969 he was Chairman of the CFR, David Rockefeller in his early 40's then took over as chairman after McCloy. Between 1954 and 1969 McCloy was a trustee of The Rockefeller Foundation. He was also President of The World Bank from 1953 to 1960, busy guy. After all this work for his masters he was made a named partner in the Rockefeller associated prominent New York law firm Milbank, Hadley, and McCloy. In that capacity he acted for the seven sisters, the leading multinational oil companies, including Exxon under Rockefeller control. The Seven Sisters were:

1. Anglo Iranian, this company was controlled by Britain, after the war the Rockefellers took 40%, leaving the British 40% and the Iranians whose oil it was, 20%.
2. Gulf Oil, later part of Chevron
3. Royal Dutch Shell
4. Standard Oil of California, now part of Chevron.
5. Standard Oil of New Jersey, now Exxon.
6. Standard Oil of New York, later became Mobil.
7. Texaco, later merged with Chevron.

McCloy was referred to as the Chairman of the American Establishment. He was an advisor to presidents from FDR to Reagan. Please note that he advised both Democrats and Republicans. As stated earlier, when it comes to presidents we have had an illusion of choice since FDR. On top of all that he served on the Warren Commission investigating the assassination of JFK. History has shown us and continues to do so, that the doors between the appointed public sector and the private banking sector are well oiled. We'll see another example of a Globalist minion serving his masters well in the public sector and being handsomely rewarded in the private sector in the segment on Viet Nam. To be clear, the law firm partnership was one private reward, the World Bank appointment the second, yes the World Bank is private, despite its euphemistic title.

Speaking of German munition makers getting a free ride so did approximately 1,600 Nazis under Operation Paperclip. Nazi scientists such as the famous Wernher von Braun, the man most directly responsible for the V-1 and V-2 rockets that indiscriminately killed thousands of British Citizens, as well as the rockets that got the U.S. to the moon, not to mention ICBM's. It was deemed that he and his fellow scientists were too valuable to go to prison. One such Nazi that helped had an award named after him called the Strughold Award. It was the most prestigious award of the Space Medicine Association. The award was retired in 2013 when it was found that Hubertus Strughold the awards namesake did medical experiments on human beings in the camps. Of all the 1,600 Nazi's that the U.S. government brought over from Germany (many of whom where leaders in the Nazi Party), only one was ever put on trial. He was found not guilty.

So the Japanese bomb Pearl, once again the mass media goes into overdrive and stirs up the American people into war frenzy. The very day after the attack thousands of young Americans enlisted. How were they to know? If I were alive at the time I may have done the same. I remember when this false flag concept was first introduced to me. I did not believe it. I loved the WW2 history that I read about in school history books, (you know, the ones that keep getting rewritten). I could tell you the strength of our forces in the battle of Midway June 4th-7th, 1942. The strength of the Japanese forces in the same battle. This false flag concept was foreign to all the studying and movies I had watched. Of course we didn't know they were coming! Our government would never do that! Live and learn.

A quick word on our government at the time. Ever heard of the Tuskegee Syphilis Experiment? From 1932 to 1972 the United States Government told 600 poor African American men they would receive free medical care to treat syphilis. 399 had the disease before the study was launched, 201 did not. The 201 unaffected were the perfect control group. They were the same race as the infected men, they were of the same socio economic level and they lived in the same area thus eliminating environmental factors to a large degree, or the largest degree possible. Instead of curing the infected men of the disease with penicillin in 1940, the U.S. Government decided it would be better to document the long term effects of Syphilis on men. It gets worse, the wife's of these men were infected as well. There were children born with congenital syphilis. The men could have been cured decades before with penicillin. So not only was the U.S. Government involved, so were the doctors who theoretically took the Hippocratic Oath. It's hard to imagine anyone, let alone the U. S. government and Doctors doing something like that…yet it is a matter of historical fact. Bill Clinton publically apologized for it at the White House in May, 1997.

Any historian will tell you that after the battle of Midway America ruled the Pacific. Not only did we destroy the flower of their navy but their best pilots were killed. They lost all four aircraft carriers in their strike force. We lost one. They lost all of their 248 carrier based planes, all of them. They lost all of their best pilots, the very ones responsible for the Pearl attack. They lost 3,057 men. We lost 307.[15] This is how nearly every land and sea battle went. The Japanese were simply overmatched. After the battle of Midway due to severe oil and gas shortages the new Japanese pilot training was severely restricted. The new pilots they had were literally blown out of the sky by American pilots with sufficient training. Why did it take 3.3 more years to conquer Japan? Here are some additional logistics when viewed from a lens of logic that make our actions in the Pacific either quite stupid or designed to keep a war going for profit. Why did japan attack us in the first place? Surely they knew they couldn't win. Admiral Yamamoto Isoruku who led the attack on Pearl and Midway told anyone who would listen that Japan had no hope in winning a war with the U. S. He had studied in the U.S. and was aware of our industrial might. It should be known that Mitsubishi manufactured the 0 aircraft, I did not say designed it. Toyota, Honda and Nissan were involved as well. You may remember Datsun changing its name to Nissan. They didn't change their name to Nissan, they changed it back to Nissan. The reason they began here under Datsun was because they thought their cars would not sell under the Nissan name because of that companies WW2 history. It's interesting to note that whether it was German or Japanese companies they all thrived after the war. The Japanese made one keel up aircraft carrier from 1941 till the end of the war. It was mechanically problematic and was sunk before it ever launched a single plan. The U. S. built 24 during the war. The U.S. aircraft carriers were superior in every way. More armor. More guns, bigger, faster and, most importantly, the planes could be raised to the flight deck all at once. The Japanese carriers did not have these capabilities. They only had space for half their planes on the flight deck. This meant that the planes launched first had to burn precious fuel while waiting above the carrier for the rest of their planes to

---

15   *National WW2 Museum> articles.*

upload and launch. The Japanese were already running out of fuel reserves. This was one of the deciding factors at Midway.

Why did we Island hop. Why did we slug it out with entrenched Japanese forces for tiny Islands? The mass media said it was to conquer the various islands to get landing strips to bomb Japan. Why? Taiwan (then called Formosa) was The United States ally in WW2. That islands proximity to Japan was well within reach of our B17 bombers introduced in 1938 as well as our B29 bombers introduced in May of 1944? The war could have been over much sooner had we simply drove the Japanese out of Taiwan and launched our bombers from there. Remember, the president is the commander and chief of the armed forces. I'm sure that Generals and Admirals suggested a more direct approach like the one I just mentioned and were not listened to. That would have shortened the war, less money to be made by old men as young men died. Why did we supply Japan oil up until the summer of 1941 when they were attacking our friend China since 1937 with some hostilities starting as early as 1931? Of course the Japanese stockpiled as much oil as they could. That means Pearl was bombed with oil supplied by none other than Rockefeller owned Standard Oil. Japan had to be perceived as a plausible antagonist in the coming planned war. How much easier to condition the American people to war then by showing them on a map a huge swath of China that Japan had conquered as well as parts of Southeast Asia. Japans domestic oil production in 1941, for the entire year equaled one day of American oil production.[16]

Where did Japan get their technology? Japan is an Island. It was a feudal society with the Emperor at the pinnacle and slightly below him where the Shoguns, provincial rulers who controlled Samurai. The Samurai controlled the peasants. The samurai held the power of life and death over a peasant. If a Samurai felt disrespected by a peasant he could literally cut off the head of the offending peasant with his Katana (Japanese long sword, the metal of which was folded over 200 times in the forge to remove impurities and create strength and flexibility). Below them were the peasants' holding it all up. There was a tiny mercantile class squeezed into the middle. This form of society had existed for millennia. Life was good, unless you were a peasant. Why would the people at the top want change or foreign influence? There were Geishas, opium and sake, and wind, string and percussion

---

16   *http:wwwhistclo/essay/war/ww2/str/w2j-oil.htmle.*

instruments. Sex, drugs and rock and roll. The Japanese were isolated from the west and its technology until Admiral Perry sailed into Tokyo Harbor at the head of gunships and forced trade. It was then interrupted by our Civil War until after 1865. The slack in trade was taken up by the masters of the seas, The British. The British Empire had the most technologically advanced navy in the world. It was the British that had the first full-length flight deck on an aircraft carrier in 1918. The imperial Japanese navy had a long standing relationship with the British Royal Navy, even displaying a lock of famed British naval commander Admiral Horatio Lord Nelson's hair at the Eta Jima Naval Academy. Japans 27 thousand ton Kongo-class battleships were designed by British naval architects, and Kongo herself was built in Britain. Therefore it is not surprising that the Japanese Navy relied heavily upon its English friends for guidance in the emerging art of aircraft carrier technology.[17] We are to believe that as late as 1865 they were fighting using swords and bow and arrows and 65 years later they were on a near technological par with the west? Social Science Japan Journal Vol. 4, NO. I, pp59-79 2001 gives us considerable insight regarding Japans ability to crawl and then literally fly. Ford, GM (DuPont Family) and GE (Morgan Family) were all in Japan in the 20's and 30's. Representatives of these companies taught the Japanese factory methods using mass produced interchangeable parts (the famous Ford Assembly Line). The article goes on to say aviation tech was also shared. GE was there to bring the Japanese up to speed on electronic tech. Their 0 fighter was actually superior to our planes until 1943. It may have been built in Japan but it was designed here in the U. S. Many WW2 veterans I spoke to say the 0 was a Jack Northrop design sold to the Japanese. Let's say that by some miracle of technological evolution the Japanese went from the bow and arrow in 1865 to submarines, battleships and aircraft carries in a few short decades. Why did there technology stop completely. There was no next generation 0 fighter plane. Their carriers did not improve, their weaponry, nothing. How about today? Japans pretty technologically advanced right? They just retrofitted their two best most advanced destroyers to carry aircraft. The power plant, GE LM2500-30 gas turbines, made in the U.S. The aircraft used on the carriers, 14 F-35B American made jets that can take off and land vertically. By contrast our carriers are 4 times the size with nuclear power capable of 15 years of use without refueling. Our carriers carry 75 plus aircraft that can actually take off and land horizontally because they are not tiny. On the other hand the

---

17   *On Wave and Wing: The 100 year quest to perfect the Aircraft Carrier. By Barrett Tillman.*

United States made serious improvements in all our war material, not to mention the A bomb. You might say the Japanese were getting bombed so they couldn't develop more tech. The Germans were getting bombed in the day by the U. S. and at night by the British as early as 1943. Despite all that they came up with the V1 and V2 rockets and the world's first jet fighter used in battle. On top of all that they were close to an A bomb as well. And sadly, why did we drop two Atomic bombs on a defeated enemy. Could it have been to see the effects of the bombs? The second more powerful than the first. We are told that the loss of life on both sides would have been horrific had we invaded the rest of the Japanese home islands after Okinawa. The reality is the Japanese had no ability left to defend themselves, no oil, no factories left standing to make bullets, nothing. On top of all that they were starving. Why not just wait them out? How about the European Front?

In terms of the length of the war in Europe the same logistical questions should be pondered. Where did Germany get its oil prior to declaring war on the U. S.? Germany got the vast majority of pre-war oil from Rockefeller owned Standard Oil. Do you think they stockpiled any of it for the future? That means again, our troops were being killed by planes and tanks fueled by their own country's oil. Some sources say that Standard oil continued to supply Germany with oil even after the U.S. entered the war. Does that sound impossible? Where then did they get it? Germany produced very little oil, certainly not enough to wage war. German controlled Romania had oil but not nearly enough for war. The Russians had oil fields but the Germans held them only briefly, three months or so and they only produced about 70 barrels a day. You get about 20 gallons of gas/diesel out of a barrel of oil. According to Charles Higham's book: Trading With the Enemy: An Expose of The Nazi-American Money Plot 1933-1949. The Germans got their oil from Standard Oil. Charles (the author) was the son of a British Member of Parliament. He drew heavily on declassified documents from the U. S. national Archives. The book documents where Germany got oil during the war, as well as tetraethyl lead. German and Japanese plans could not fly without it. The only sources of tetraethyl lead were Standard Oil, Du Pont and General Motors which was owned by the Du Pont family at that time. The Du Pont family supplied 40% of munitions in WW1 and a huge amount in WW2. In those days the family was called the merchants of death. Like Balzac said "Behind every great fortune lies a crime." The book also goes on to document that Chase Bank (Rockefeller Bank) continued to do business with Nazi Germany during the war. Not to be left out, the

House of Morgan was there too, as well as the Ford Motor Co. Standard oil had $120 million invested, Gm $35 million, ITT $30 million and Ford $17 million. These figures are in 1940's dollars. In 1939 when Germany and Russia attacked Poland and divided the country, why is it that France and England declared war on Germany but not Russia? France, England and Poland had a specific, detailed military alliance in place. Hmm. When you look at war footage showing the D Day landing. Why were our men being dropped off in landing craft directly in front of pill boxes (steel and concrete fortified bunkers with Germans inside with very large machine guns)? Why didn't our ships carrying the landing craft go where the enemy was not? They did when Theodore Roosevelt Jr. (Teddy's son) was on board. Apparently they were blown off course. His ships landed a mile south of their objective where the Germans were not. Theodore was able to walk about on the beach with a cane and a pistol. He was 56 at the time, the oldest man to land at Normandy. I'm not picturing him dodging bullets with the help of his cane. He won the Medal of Honor for his efforts landing in the wrong spot. Lastly, let's not forget about the British Empire at the time. We are led to believe that tiny England held out all alone before we came to help them. England at that time was called The British Empire. It held de facto political and economic control over 25% of the world population and 30% of its land mass. Some of these areas of control included India with a huge population, Canada with oil, Australia, South Africa and New Zealand. Germany and Japan never had a prayer. International bankers don't start and prolong wars when they are not sure of the outcome. How could they be so sure? In this case, simply cutting off oil supplies. We could go on and on. I think the point has been made, longer war, more money.

One more point on WW2. Where did the utterly destroyed countries of Germany and Japan get the money and material to rebuild? Their governments had no money. Germany and Japan borrowed yet more money from the international banking families that pulled the strings all along. Chase bank was the first non-German bank to open in post war Germany. That is from J.P. Morgan's website. The survivors of those countries and their descendants are still paying it back. The wooden buildings made by true craftsmen full of grace and beauty that made up Tokyo before the war, these were replaced by American designed and built skyscrapers with no elegance, no Shibumi. There is nothing Japanese about them. Conquered people unfortunately lose their culture.

Iran

In the July 1, 2019 issue of Time magazine some truth came out. I was shocked! You may remember how I feel about that rag, Time Magazine. The article said: Washington deposed Iran's last freely elected leader, then kept on meddling. The deposed leader was Mohammad Mosaddegh. This was the first CIA led coup to depose a foreign leader. The CIA man behind the coup has a familiar last name, Roosevelt. His name was Kermit Roosevelt Jr., he was the grandson of President Teddy Roosevelt. He came before the frog. His dad was a CFR member as was Theodore Roosevelt IV. As a result of this coup the Shaw came to power. The democracy was gone. The oilfields of Iran were free for plunder by America and Britain. The Shaw got rich and everyone was happy…except a lot of the people of Iran. This lack of sharing the country's wealth with its own citizens led to the rise of the Ayatollah Khomeini and the infamous American hostage crisis. Remember the pickup trucks with Mickey Mouse giving the finger to Iran. Americans were mad. They were mad at Iran because the Globalist controlled media never let them know that The Globalists caused it all! Iran (Persia until 1935) had a proud Heritage, they would not be under anyone's thumb. What you see happening in the Middle East today is a result of Globalist meddling in Iran. The CFR/Globalist coup of 1954 is giving us dividends of war, famine, disease and the threat of Nuclear War. Benjamin Netanyahu has been saying for years how close Iran is to having a Nuclear Bomb. If he is saying it, bank on it. The Mossad (Israel's secret service) is probably the best in the world, they have to be, it's about their nation's very survival. The Iranian leadership has said they want to wipe Israel off the face of the Earth. With Israel being our ally that's not real swell for the U. S. I am not saying the Iranian people are bad or are warmongers. I have friends that are Persian. I'm saying the leadership that the Globalists propelled into power by their meddling are nut jobs. Anyone remember Ahmadinejad? He was president of Iran from 2005 till 2013. He is a Shiite that believes in the coming Mahdi. The Mahdi will appear in the end times and make all well with the world. The catch is he will only appear if there is terrible chaos going on in the world. Ahmadinejad wanted to hasten his arrival by creating chaos. Had the Globalists not interfered in Iran in 1954 it's probable that Ahmadinejad would never have come to power. These Globalists are not the people we want running a world government. This is the mess they created for President Trump to deal with, and that's just the Middle East. The three countries with the caravans coming to our border (Guatemala.

Honduras and El Salvador) . These country's also experienced Globalist meddling, that's why they're train wrecks. We've been lending them money for decades. When they can't pay it back we lend them even more. Doesn't make much since does it. The next chapter on The Federal Reserve will make this clear.

When speaking of the early CIA and the first coup in Iran we've got to mention the Dulles brothers, both CFR members. You've heard of Dulles International Airport outside of D.C. It is named after John Dulles, Allen's older brother. John Dulles was U. S. Secretary of State from 1953 to 1959. Allen Dulles, April, 1893-january, 1969. Allen was the longest serving head of the CIA. 1953-1961. Incidentally George H. W. Bush was also the head of the CIA from January, 1976- January, 1977. It was during Allen Dulles' tenure as Director of the CIA that the Iranian coup transpired. He was also instrumental in setting up a program called MKULTRA or as some call it MK ULTRA. MKULTRA was the CIA's first foray into mind control in 1953. The program used LSD in an attempt to control people's minds. In the programs early stages experiments were conducted on army personnel without their knowledge. In its later stages it was expanded to include American citizens. It worked like this. San Francisco prostitutes were paid to slip their "clients" LSD. The effects on these men were then monitored by CIA operatives via two way mirrors. The CIA operatives were not trained scientists. The doctor administering the program, Sidney Gottlieb was himself using the drug during the ten years this secret program was being funded by our tax dollars. The subjects were often locked in rooms in straightjackets while loud music continually played on a loop. That in my mind falls under the torture category. Article 17, paragraph 4 of the 1949 Geneva Convention states the following: No physical or mental torture, nor any form of coercion, may be inflicted on prisoners of war to secure from them information of any kind whatever. I guess Allen Dulles thought it was ok to torture American citizens. This is a matter of historic fact.

Allen wasn't done yet. He also oversaw the 1954 Guatemalan coup. The CIA under Allen Dulles deposed the democratically elected president Jacobo Arbenz. The CIA then installed the military dictatorship of Carlos Castillo Armas, the first in a long line of U.S. backed rulers in Guatemala. The U. S. Secretary of state at the time, Allen's big brother John, was also involved. This coup led to widespread torture of freedom fighters and genocide of the Maya peoples. As many as 200,000 people simply disappeared. The new

U. S. backed dictator (Armas) outlawed political parties and trade unions. All of this led to a four decade civil war with a long line of U. S. backed dictators. One of the reasons we were there…fruit. This is where the term banana republic comes from. In March of 1999 Bill Clinton apologized to the Guatemalan government for the atrocities committed by U. S. backed dictatorships. Allen Dulles was instrumental in the failed Bay of Pigs disaster shortly after that. He was dismissed by JFK shortly thereafter. After the assassination of JFK, Allen severed on the Warren Commission that investigated the assassination. That seems like a conflict of interest to me, how about you? It's no wonder that President Trump refers to Washington as the swamp. Nothing ever changes because American citizens keep believing the Globalist controlled media. The Eastern Establishment is alive and well. The Dulles boy's grandfather was U. S. secretary of State under Harrison and their uncle was U. S. Secretary of State under Wilson. Just think, if you and your brother overthrow a couple countries and cause economic hardship for those countries people, put billions of dollars in already rich men's pocket's and cause the death of millions, you can get an airport named after you!

Viet Nam

Your Globalist controlled history books and media will tell you that the Viet Nam war was because of the Gulf of Tonkin Incident. The fiction goes like this: On August 4th 1964 Vietnamese torpedo boats attacked U. S. navy destroyer Maddox while in international waters. This was the primary reason for the Viet Nam war. Another false flag event. The problem is it never happened! This bit of fiction spun by CFR member and Secretary of State Robert S. McNamara lead to the Gulf of Tonkin Resolution and the Vietnam War. The resolution authorized the chief executive to take all necessary measures to repel any armed attack against the United States and to prevent further aggression. This resolution effectively nullified our system of checks and balances. No congressional oversight was necessary. CFR member President Johnson was delighted. Regarding the resolution Johnson said "it was like grandma's nightshirt, It covered everything.[18] The above referenced article is based on 200 documents declassified by the NSA in 2005 and 2006. McNamara was rewarded handsomely. He became the first none family member to head the Ford Corporation and then became

---

18   *U. S. Naval Institute, The Truth About Tonkin by Lieutenant Commander Pat Patterson, U. S. Navy. The reader can find this at usni.org.*

the head of the World Bank. When the war was going the backlash in the U.S. was such that it nearly ripped the country apart. The narrative by the Globalists then became; we've got to keep the world safe for democracy. This is 15 years after the CIA/CFR coup that deposed a Democratic government in Iran. The domino theory was trotted out. If we don't stop communism there, all of Southeast Asia will fall to communism one by one. So here are American young men fresh out of high school being drafted to go fight in Vietnam, a place most could not find on a map. I thought only Congress could declare war? How then were our young men drafted? A few logical questions. We are to believe that the mightiest country on Earth couldn't beat the North Vietnamese Army, even with help from the South Vietnamese? Why didn't we bomb their supply lines, ports and manufacturing centers? We knew where their war material came from…bomb it. Our Generals were not allowed to. Remember the President is the commander and chief. LBJ and latter Nixon would not allow it. It gets worse. The Soviet Union was involved as was the UN. The Soviet Union at the time was part of the UN general council. When American Generals drew up battle plans the plans were made known to the UN, and thus the Soviets. The Soviets then informed the North Vietnamese Army who were then able to melt away into the jungle before American troops could engage them. Professor Antony Sutton (1925-2002) of Stanford University and the Hoover Institute was an early conspiracy theorist. His books are amazing and as a professor, well documented. In National Suicide, Military Aid to The Soviet Union, he informs us of the fact that many of the weapons supplied for the North Vietnamese Army were from American built and funded factories in the USSR. The end result of the war: 58,220 Americans dead, 300,000 plus wounded. As far as Vietnam? It became 100% communist. The American tax payer? Billions more in debt to the international bankers and families ripped asunder.

The effects of the war are being felt in ways you'll never here about from the Globalist media. Agent Orange was a defoliate used in Viet Nam from 1961 to 1971. It was manufactured by Dow Chemical and Monsanto. Monsanto makes lots and lots of genetically modified seeds for your food. When we think of the effects of Agent Orange we think in terms of our fighting men. Unfortunately health problems attributable to Agent Orange are being found in not only our soldier's kids but their grandchildren as well.[19] Monsanto

---

19   *Veterans affairs (.gov) According to popularresistance.org,.*

partnered with G. D. Searle in the 70's. Searle faked over 100 studies that clamed aspartame to be safe. The FDA initiates a grand jury investigation for "knowingly misrepresenting findings and concealing material facts and making false statements" in regard to aspartame. So what does Monsanto's partner do? They tap CFR member Donald Rumsfeld, Secretary of Defense under both Ford and George W. Bush as their new CEO. Rumsfeld flexes his political muscle and voila, Aspartame is approved by the FDA and is in over 5,000 products you eat. It is a known carcinogen.

911

I was in Downey, California when I was rushed to a TV where I could see the planes flying into the two towers of the world trade center. I then saw the towers come straight down. My first thought was, that looks like a controlled demolition I've seen on TV when one of the Las Vegas hotel/casinos had seen its day. The more I watched it the more convinced I became it was a controlled demolition. Then the reports of firefighters at the scene hearing explosions from below started coming out. Then, months later documentaries started coming out. Some were very good. Now we have the following source: Architects and Engineers for 911 Truth.org. We have 3,000 plus architects, demolition experts and engineers saying the towers could not have come down that way. They all say the same thing, no way had the towers come down because of the planes. The thing about architects and engineers is they do a lot of math. Math is pure logic. Math is hard for a lot of people. These guys chose to make a career out of math. I'm pretty sure these people are quite smart. They know the weight bearing loads of the steel used in the construction of the towers. The temperature at which the steel girders used to hold the building up burn at. They can do the math on the speed and weight of the planes that hit the building. The math doesn't add up. They are not conspiracy theorists, they are just calling foul when they see it. It was Dick Cheney who opposed an investigation into the collapse of the Towers. His stated reason was it would take resources away from the "war on Terror." The investigation was delayed for one year. It was Haliburton (Dick Cheney's involvement in that company a bit alter) that profited so handsomely when we went into Afghanistan. Immediately after the towers came down experts in demolition were saying it was definitely a controlled explosion. The towers remain the only steel framed buildings in history to come down as a supposed result of fire. There was molten steel found at the bottom of the rubble. The problem is aircraft fuel does not burn hot enough to melt the steel girders holding up the building. It is the evidence of molten steel that is impossible as a result of fire that simply cannot be explained away in terms of science. Many experts say the molten steel is evidence of an explosion or multiple explosions as some fire fighters claimed. Incidentally, the firefighters were put under a gag order, for national security of course. So what we have is another False Flag event. We'll get to the two main things that the Globalists got out of it in a moment. First know that the four most important members of the 911 Investigative Commission are/were all CFR members. Chairman Thomas Kean, Vice-Chairman LEE Hamilton, Executive director Philip Zelikow (who was the person who decided what evidence would be presented to the members of the commission and what would be withheld from them) and Deputy Executive Director Christopher Kojh. The Patriot Act and the war in Afghanistan and Iraq are the results of 911…other than thousands of Americans dying and many brave first responders that survived with cancer. The Patriot Act became effective October 26, 2001. It's amazing how fast the government can move when it's time to squash Americans rights. Some sources say the act was already printed and ready to go. The two constitutional amendments most directly impacted by the Patriot Act were the 1st and the 4th. The first Amendment reads like this. Congress shall make no law respecting an establishment of religion, or prohibiting the free exercise thereof, or abridging the freedom of speech, or the press, or the right of the people to peaceably assemble. And to petition the Government for redress of grievances. The 4th reads like this. The right of the people to be secure in their persons, houses, papers and effects, against unreasonable searches and seizures, shall not be violated, and no Warrants shall issue, but upon reasonable cause, supported by Oath or affirmation, and particularly describing the place to be searched, and the persons or things to be seized. These two amendments can be nullified in the event of a National Emergency or if you are merely accused of being a terrorist. Upon being falsely accused your first and fourth amendment rights would go right out of the window. This is scary stuff. What did the American people do a few years later? We elected Bush for another 4 year term. The Globalists learned a long time ago that control of the media is key, and unfortunately the voting public can be made to believe anything. They have no respect for our collective intelligence. Based on everything we've let them get away with can you blame them?

Any halfway decent source will tell you Afghanistan has estimates of upwards of 1 trillion dollars' worth of rare earth minerals in its soil. We also would like to build a huge oil pipeline through it. Iraq has oil. The war in Afghanistan has been going on since 911. The monetary cost as President Trump says is 8 trillion. The death toll, 2,400 Americans (if that number doesn't sound very large to you, it is if you lost a loved one), 24,000 Afghan civilians and 62,000 Afghan soldiers. The war in Iraq went on from 2003 till 2011, we still have soldiers there. According to the Iraq Body Count Program, 150,000 Iraqis died violent deaths. What has changed? American national debt and the Islamic worlds feeling toward us. By being there we are breeding hatred. Here's a scenario. I'm an Afghan or Iraqi man. I'm between 18 and 25. My testosterone levels are thru the roof. A U. S. drone just accidentally killed my little brother. I just became radicalized. I'm now looking for the first terrorist cell I can join to kill Americans. This is how wars self-perpetuate. So we have young men dying and old men getting richer. We had a Globalist Republican President get us in to Afghanistan and Iraq and a Globalist Democratic President keep us in. We've all heard of Halliburton right. Dick Cheney, George W. Bush's vice president and George H. W. Bush's secretary of defense was a director of the CFR. He was called the most powerful VP in history. He was also the CEO of Halliburton from 1995 until 2000. Halliburton has a 100 year history. They are into oil wells (think Deep Water Horizon and the catastrophe that was), logistics and construction for U. S. troops all over the world and much more. None of it pretty. The company has been the focus of litigation on an ongoing bases for decades. The company and its subsidiaries are so corrupt that there is a website devoted to exposing the corruption. The website is Halliburtonwatch.org. The following information comes from the site. 1992, then secretary of defense Dick Cheney is instrumental in awarding Brown & Root a Halliburton subsidiary a $2.2 billion contract to provide logistics for the U. S. Army Corps of Engineers in the Balkans. In 1995, without any previous business experience, Cheney leaves the Department of Defense and becomes CEO of Halliburton. Under Cheney's leadership the company go's from number 73rd to 18th on the pentagon's list of top contractors. In 1996, Halliburton's subsidiary European Marine Contractors help lay a pipeline in Burma. Several human rights groups allege human rights violations including murder, torture and rape perpetrated by the soldiers in the pay of Halliburton's subsidiary to protect the pipeline. I'm pretty sure that's a private army...like drug cartels have. In 1997, Cheney contributes to Project for the New American Century (nice euphemism). The group advocates for the removal of Saddam Hussein's regime as early as January 1998. That same year even with the Iran-Libya sanctions in place

Halliburton continues to do business in Iran. It pays a mere $15,000 fine to settle the allegations but admits no wrong doing and continues to do business in Iran and Libya throughout Cheney's tenure as CEO. By the time Cheney left in 2000, Halliburton had yearly revenues of $15 billion and is now the largest diversified energy services, engineering, construction and maintenance company in the world. There is so much information available on Halliburtionwatch.org that I strongly recommend the interested reader to spend some time there. So Cheney is involved in all this Quid Pro Quo and you here nothing. President Trump offers his Hotel at cost to the G7 and he's an axe murderer. The Globalists control what you hear and read. How about Joe Biden's son Hunter? Same Quid Pro Quo with China as Cheney in numerous countries, and how did the Globalist media report on it? One interview on one channel and that's it. How about the book and Documentary Clinton Cash by: Peter Schweizer. Here is a very quick synopsis. Bill Clinton's speaking fees went up as much as ten times what he was paid before Hillary became Secretary of State. When he spoke in various countries in some instances the Clinton Global Initiative was then paid millions and a deal was done as Hillary happened to coincidentally be in that country at the same time. Uranium 1 is one such deal. As a result of Uranium 1 Russia received mining rights to 20% of the United States Uranium. Does that sound like Russian collusion to you? Reports also came out that only 10% of the charitable founds paid to the CGI made it to charities. Hillary is on record stating that they left the white house not only broke but in debt. They are now worth a reported 130 million. I believe that do be an extremely low estimate. On top of all that the people they did their nefarious business with were not people you'd invite to Sunday dinner. Some were dictators with human rights records that even the Globalist UN had to speak out against for appearance sake. If you take an hour to watch the free video on your phone or computer you will realize why women and men alike wear shirts that say "Hillary for Prison." They should say Hillary and Bill for prison.

"America does not need to see the tax returns of a billionaire that became a public servant...America needs to see the tax returns of public servants who became millionaires while being public servants."Unknown writer.

At the beginning of this chapter I had three stated goals. Enlighten the reader about past deeds of evil attributable to the CFR, convince you the reader we don't want these people running a One World Government (in case you're naïve enough to think that could be a good thing)and illuminate the reader to the media's partnership and culpability. To be crystal clear, I do not think or believe that all news anchors and writers from the news stations and the print organizations I've mentioned in the proceeding pages have knowledge that their employer is part of the Globalism push. Amy Robach certainly doesn't by her own admission. She was recently caught on a hot mic with the cameras rolling and stated that, "I've had this story for three years…and we would not put it on the air." "We had Clinton, we had everything." She is speaking of the Jeffery Epstein scandal. She says she had a witness and victim of abuse that was in hiding for years and was going to tell all. She goes on to say that ABC would not go forward with the story because of pressure from the palace, the palace, being Buckingham Palace. Prince Andrew was implicated in the story. My English friends tell me that Prince Andrew is called Randy Andy in the U. K. He was photographed with Epstein after Epstein's conviction for which he received a slap on the rist. Clinton's people said he was on the plane 4 times, the flight manifest shows 27. The planes nickname was The Lolita Express. The private Island's nickname, Orgy Island. Amy Robach goes on to say that pressure was put on ABC in a million different ways and that ABC was afraid to air the story. That ABC was more interested in a Harry and Megan Interview. Let's apply some logic, from a ratings point of view which one do you think would have made the network more money? Harry's uncle, Randy Andy and Bill Clinton caught in a he sexual scandal or Harry's choice of baby clothes? No pressure was put on ABC to not run the story, none was needed, it doesn't work that way. A globalist at ABC simply made a decision not to run the story because it was bad for the Royals and bad for Hillary's campaign for president. Amy Robach goes on to say that she absolutely believes Epstein was murdered. This story aired on Fox as well as OANN. Those stations got the story from Project Veritas. ABC had to comment on why they did not air the story. Their comment: ABC News denied it tried to stop Robach's story, claiming it did not "meet our standards to air." The same station that tried to paint President Trump in a

bad light for keeping a campaign promise and beginning the Syria withdrawal? How'd they do it? They showed footage of a gun range in Kentucky where they were doing an annual, controlled, "blow up lots of stuff night."ABC showed footage of the gun range while the explosions were going off and claimed it was Syria as a result of President Trump removing our soldiers. The footage was from years ago. How does someone make that mistake? ABC was caught because someone from the gun range saw the footage and spoke out and up. The same "standards to air" that lambasted Brett Kavanagh day after day for weeks?

As I write this chapter two weeks of the impeachment inquiry have just ended. Ostensibly they were all about Quid Pro Quo. The inquiry alleges President Trump was withholding United States military aid to Ukraine unless Ukraine dug up dirt on CFR member Joe Biden. Shortly after the unfounded allegation was made the President of Ukraine came out and said President Trump did not ask him for anything. In a sane world that should have been the end of it. Given the fact that President Trump is undoing decades of Globalist work and planning, the impeachment inquiry went forward. Why did the Democratic congress people go along with it, Self-preservation. They know that their seats are that much more vulnerable as a Republican president becomes more and more popular and more and more democratic seats become more vulnerable to republicans. I know the Republican Party lost congressional seats in the first election after Trump became President. That is a historical statistic. Republican President, Republican Senate = loss of seats in congress. What is not historical is how few were lost. What's the old saying, "It's the economy stupid." So here we go with the inquiry. While in the middle of it Time magazine's November 18th, 2019 issue reads in huge red letters: The Impeachment of Donald Trump. It's not an impeachment it's an inquiry. Time magazine bombards their readers with subliminal messages like this on a constant basis. Not to be outdone George Stephanopoulos is then heard every morning breathlessly describing today's bombshell testimony. He makes me laugh. If you listen to different news you would have seen on camera with full audio, live and in person at the inquiry, Ohio Representative Jim Jordon taking said testimony apart like a cardboard box. There is nothing there. Every political analyst not a hater of President Trump is saying the same thing. Then there's Texas Representative John Ratcliffe. This guy doesn't waste time (or tax payer dollars) he goes right to the jugular. He says to the witness, the one with the bombshell testimony according to George S. and says, "Where is the impeachable offence in that call." The answer, silence, nothing, nada. The question was asked of the two bombshell witnesses. This impeachment inquiry was a desperate attempt to smear President Trump with the hope the mere appearance of wrong doing will garner the Desperate Democrats votes. I want to be clear, I do not think more than half of congress are Globalists. I do think that many congress people are more interested in keeping their jobs than doing their jobs. For evidence I would point to the USMCA deal that has been on Nancy Pelosi's desk for nearly a year. No wonder President Trump calls them the do nothing democrats.

I have some Quid Pro Quo for you. How about Joe Biden being caught on camera at the CFR headquarters bragging about what he did in Ukraine. Joe was sitting at the "Masters of the World" hangout. Perhaps that was why he was so bold, call it showing off. He is speaking of the Ukrainian prosecutor investigating Burisma, the company his inexperienced, unqualified son, with zero experience in the field was made a board member of. He says "We had a billion dollar loan guarantee, I leave in 6 hours, if that prosecutor is not fired you're not getting the money. "Well son of a bitch, he got fired." Sound like Quid Pro Quo to you? Nothing about this on ABC, CBS, NBC, CNN or MSNBC. Nothing in Time Magazine, the New York Times or the Washington Post. I'll say it again, our news is controlled. You can hear Joe speaking for yourself. Just key in Biden brags at the CFR.

President Trump did have CFR member, Rex Tillerson, as the United States Secretary of State. Rex soon heard the immortal words, "you're fired." Gerome Powell is a CFR member as well. Presidents Trump's comment on him "you can't win them all". President Trump did get Powell to reduce interest rates in late 2019. I believe we will be seeing a running battle between the two of them until Powel is somehow gotten out of the position as Federal Reserve Chairman. John Bolton is also a CFR member. He is just wrote an anti-Trump book. So why did President Trump put the three in office? Maybe Tillerson fooled him and convinced President Trump that he was one of the good ones. Regarding Powell and Bolton, maybe they too convinced President Trump that they were good. It is interesting to note that Powell was heard on TV saying, "He can't fire me." He was speaking of president Trump. Regarding the Fed, As Churchill said about Russia, it is a riddle, wrapped in a mystery, inside an enigma. Again we'll get to the Fed next.

I honestly believe that President Trump did not know the depth of the swamp. I do not think he read books such as these. When you're running a company that does business all over the world, in different time zones, you don't have time to read books like these. Many of the books I've drawn from for this text are quite hard to find. The information on the net, easy. You just have to know what you are looking for.

The biggest problem the Globalists are having is your smart phone and computer. For the last three years internet freedom has been under attack, and censorship worldwide has increased. 90% of the news you hear or read is controlled by 6 corporations. The internet allows you to look up any news subject and find dissenting, non-Globalist facts. Often times, those who the fake news is covering for are caught on film lying. You will never hear it on the fake news identified earlier. Hillary had something interesting to say about the internet in February, 2020. This was reported on Fox's The Five. She said don't believe the internet, it is the biggest threat to democracy. I'm wondering how knowledge can be a threat to democracy. Keep in mind that totalitarian governments such as China and Iran are constantly censoring internet access. I assure you the DPRK (Democratic People's Republic of Korea) has zero unapproved internet access. With that thought in mind what does that tell you about Hillary telling you the internet is going to destroy democracy? The Globalists are awakened to the threat. Many current members of the CFR no longer appear on the membership rosters. Nancy Pelosi and Adam Schiff do not appear on current rosters but have spoken and been seen at the council many times, you can key in Nancy Pelosi or Adam Schiff speak at the CFR on your phone or computer and hear them babel if you like. Their agenda certainly suggests that they are Globalists. Think about Adam Schiff. He wants to get rid of a president that has made our economy explode with wealth and is getting our soldiers out of endless foreign wars, like the 19 year war in Afghanistan that has cost and estimated 8 trillion dollars. If he were a patriot he would not be doing and saying what he does. Consider the beginning of the impeachment trial. Since the rules of the senate allowed Schiff to make his argument for 24 uninterrupted hours, it gave him the opportunity to frame the case against President Trump in fully partisan and factually deficient terms. The only word that accurately describes what Schiff did to President Trump in his presentation of the case is to say he framed him. To use a legal term of art, Schiff argued "facts not in evidence," and without anyone to object the senators were left to assume that the facts were true when time and again they were false and misleading.[20] Unfortunately ABC, CBS, NBC, MSNBC and CNN all made sure that the above "facts" were heard by you, the American people. Upon being called out on his outright lies Schiff claimed what he said was a parody of President Trumps phone call with Ukraine. He said all this after president Trump released the transcript of the call. You know and I know

20   Real Clear Politics.

that Schiff, Pelosi and Schumer went over that Ukraine call transcript with a fine toothed comb before Schiff spoke. When Schiff recited his "parody" he was simply lying, pure, simple, and ugly. There are countries waking up. The country not experiencing this problem, Iceland. Iceland recently overthrew its entire government. All of it. Any of you remember hearing about that in the Globalist controlled media? In an article titled, Icelanders Overthrow Government and Rewrite Constitution After Banking Fraud, there was no word from U. S. Media, by Rebecca Savastio. The article states that there are accusations of a U.S. cover-up. That the U. S. media ignored this monumental, unprecedented development in a prosperous European country. The article goes on to state that this information is available by a simple search on Google. There is so much information at your fingertips. Find a good news station or website and see how what they say differs from what you are being indoctrinated with. You can do it with your phone a lot of the time. That's what I did regarding California Governor Gavin Newsome. As it turns out he founded the PlumpJack Group with Gordon Getty. It encompasses 23 businesses including wineries, restaurants and hotels.[21] Gordon Getty is the heir to the Getty Oil fortune. You may have heard of the Getty Museum in Southern California. Interesting that the most socialistic governor California has ever seen is in business with the super-rich. Following the money is always enlightening. I'd also like to make you aware that Gavin Newsome is related to Nancy Pelosi, and we wonder what happened to California.

So what do we know about the New World Order to enslave us all. We have a former first lady, U.S. Senator and Secretary of State telling us who tells her and the government how to think about the future. We have the son of one of the creators of the United States Federal Reserve and the CFR, Paul Warburg, with the brass to tell the Senate Foreign Relations committee "We shall have one world government whether or not you like it, either by conquest or consent." We have the head of the most powerful family in the United States, David Rockefeller, admitting to his and his family's culpability and control. We have an Ivy League Professor at Georgetown, Caroll Quigley, and mentor to Bill Clinton who studied the Globalist's documents for two years telling us this is happening and writing a 1,300 plus page book about it. We have a former U. S. Admiral and CFR member Chester Ward doing the same. We have Otto Von Bismarck expressing fear of bankers

---

21   Market Watch Magazine, August 27th 2018.

shortly after the American civil war. We have Professor Antony Sutton of Stanford University writing numerous books about The New World Order as well. This is real.

To be crystal clear this New World Order will not be a democracy. Third world nations will not rise to the living standards of first world nations. The opposite will happen. First world nations will descend and become third world nations, until finally, there are no nations. You will not have freedom of religion, private property, freedom to travel, freedom of speech, due process, or the right to reproduce unless the Globalists need more workers. In short we will all be slaves, except those who have been culpable in the Globalists One World Government plans.

I was speaking to a friend of mine the other day who is a Professor at a University in Pennsylvania. I was telling her about this book and the Globalists plans for a one world government. She said, "Why would that be so bad." I hope the preceding chapters' answered that question. Let's think of it in biblical terms. Adam and Eve were put into the Garden of Eden. Eden was paradise on this earth, no cloths needed as the weather was constant and the temperature was perfect. When Adam or Eve were hungry they merely reached out their hand for fruit that was both pleasing to the eye and good for food. They did not have to work and there was no death. They could converse with God and were created in his image. Imagine how perfect their physical appearance must have been. With that in mind do you think they may have known each other in the biblical sense before they were expelled…of course they did. They were human right. Here's the point: Adam and Eve were expelled from the garden, not Adam, Eve and little Jr. Within nine months mankind with God given freedom of choice screwed up paradise. How long do you think it'll take the Globalists?

We need: The Great Awakening.

We can't talk about the CFR without a bit of information on the Bilderbergers.

"It is difficult to re-educate people who have been brought up on nationalism to the idea of relinquishing part of their sovereignty to a supra-national body." Prince Bernard of the Netherlands.

"Today, Americans would be outraged if UN troops entered Los Angeles to restore order; tomorrow, they will be grateful. This is especially true if they were told there was an outside threat from beyond, whether real or promulgated, that threatened our very existence. It is then that all the people of the world will plead with world leaders to deliver them from this evil. The one thing every man fears is the unknown. When presented with this scenario, individual rights will be willingly relinquished for the guarantee of their well-being granted to them by their world government." Henry Kissinger, speaking in Evian, France at the 1992 Bilderberger meeting.[22]

As I earlier stated the Bilderbergers are the most powerful of the Globalist groups. They are so secret we do not know if they have a name and what it is. We call them the Bilderbergers because it is the name of the prestigious Bilderberg Hotel where they first met in 1954. They met at the behest of Prince Bernhard of the Netherlands. Most people have never heard of them. They typically meet once a year for three days and discuss what's going to happen in the world. It then happens. You hear nothing about them because they and their fellow Globalists control what you read in the paper and what you see on TV, on a global scale. Let's apply some logic. If the media was honest and doing their jobs wouldn't we hear about 120 of the most powerful people in the world meeting for three days a year, every year? We hear nothing. I like what Jim Marrs had to say about it. "I don't think 120 of the most powerful people in the world are there to talk about their golf game." No one golfs there. The meetings are held in English. Before the guests arrive the staff is replaced by non-English speakers. The rooms are debugged every morning. The perimeter of whatever 5 star hotel they completely buy out is patrolled by private security with machine guns. The inner most circle of the CFR, Tri-Lateral Commission, Club of Rome and The Royal Institute for International Affairs attend. The Club of Rome and The Royal Institute for International Affairs can be thought of as the CFR's Europeans cousins with the same goals in mind. The heads of European Central Banks, the IMF (International Monetary Fund, The World Bank and of course the past and present heads of our central bank, The Federal Reserve, they all attend. Kings and Queens as well. The Bilderbergers do allow guests. Many U.S. presidents and European prime ministers and presidents have attended before they were "elected" into office. Except president Trump. When you control the media and the money, you control public

22   the Bilderberger Group, by Daniel Estulin, page 85-86.

thought and opinion. When the meetings are in the U. S. they are usually hosted by the Rockefeller Family. There is a great picture in Daniel Estulin's book, The Bilderberg group. Someone with a camera with a great lens was able to snap some shots of the zoo animals at a meeting. You had all these titans of industry walking around with name tags on. Even easily recognized and well known people like Henry Kissinger were dutifully wearing their name tags. The person who was not wearing a name tag, David Rockefeller. When the meetings are held in Europe usually The Rothschild Family or one of the Royal Families play host. A quick word on the Rothschild family before we go on. You simply can't have a "New World Order" as George H. W. bush put it, without them. The family rose to prominence under Mayer Amschel Rothschild (1744-1812) from Germany. He had 5 sons. They each established banks in different European cities. London, Naples, Vienna, Frankfort and Paris. They became so powerful that the family was elevated to the rank of noble. Professor Guigley tells us on page 51 of his book Tragedy and Hope, that the Rothschild male decedents married first cousins and in some cases nieces for at least two generations. The Rothschild's give a whole new meaning to keeping the money in the family. Emmanuel Macron the current president of France was a Rothschild banker. He is also the youngest man elected to lead modern France. Upon seeing "one" of the Rothschild's Chateaus, Wilhelm 1 stated "A king couldn't afford this. It could only belong to a Rothschild". Wilhelm 1 was the first German Emperor (1797-1888). So the Power of the Rothschild family go's back a couple hundred years. An agent of the Rothschild family was instrumental in the forming of The Federal Reserve of the United States. Many believe them to be the most powerful family in the world. Speaking of the Rothschilds, These are the powerful forces that President Trump is fighting against every day. I've kept this section on the Bilderbergers brief. With the election of Donald Trump, the United States of America is not currently beholden to them other than the train wrecks they created prior to his election, such as NAFTA.

"Our job is not to give people what they want, but what we decide they ought to have". Former president of CBS News, Richard Salant.

I would like you to know the names of past Bilderberger attendees from the U. S. Media. We can start with Michael Bloomberg who is as of January, 2020, throwing 500 million dollars of his own money toward his presidential campaign. You have of course heard of Bloomberg news. Bloomberg News is in 72 countries and 146 news bureaus worldwide. It seems to me that if you are reporting/making news worldwide there is a bit of a conflict of interest when running for President of the United States. The Globalists are correct in their belief that Joe Biden can't get the job done without help, so we now have Michael throwing his hat in the ring.

In no particular order her are some past and present heads of the fake news media who have attended Bilderberger meetings. This information comes to us from Daniel Estulins's international bestseller, The True Story of the Bilderberger Group. Sharon Percy Rockefeller, WETA-TV president and CEO; Paul Gigot, editorial page editor of the Wall Street Journal; Osborn Elliot, former Newsweek editor; Anatole Grunwald, former editor and chief of Time and a CFR member; Joseph C. Harsch, former NBC commenter and CFR member; Gerald Piel, former chairman of Scientific American and CFR member; Peter Jennings, former anchor and senior editor of ABC's World News Tonight (now we have George Stephanopoulos); Willian Kristol, editor and publisher of the Weekly Standard magazine; Peter Job, Reuters CEO Kenneth Whyte, editor of The National Post; Donald C. Cook, former European diplomatic correspondent for the Los Angeles Times and CFR member. Leslie Stahl CBS correspondent; David Brinkley of ABC; Tom Brokaw and Dan Rather; Fareed Zakaria, editor at large for Time magazine, he also has his own show on CNN, he is also a paid columnist for the Washington Post and editor for Newsweek, also a CFR member.

Woe to those who call evil good and good evil, who put darkness for light and light for darkness, who put bitter for sweet and sweet for bitter. Isaiah 5:20 NIV of the Holy Bible.

Have you noticed how many editors of both print and TV news there are attending these meetings? Editors are the people that give the ok as to what appears in print and what you see on your big screen.

In 1976 Gary Allen informed us that the Rockefeller family had controlling interests in ABC, CBS and NBC. Daniel Estulin says the same thing in his 2005 book mentioned above. But wait you say, Disney owns ABC, yes they do. That means the Rockefellers control Mickey. Let's have a quick look at what Disney owns. This will give us an indication of how few multi-national corporations control what you see on TV, what you read and as importantly, the subtle propaganda your children and yourselves are unknowingly exposed to. Disney owns the following: ABC, 80% of ESPN, The History

Channel, 50% of A and E, FX, 60% of Hulu, Touchstone Pictures, Marvel Studios, Lucas Film, Fox Studios, Pixar. It is estimated that Disney controls 40% of the films you see at the movie theater.

Let's think of their subtle propaganda. Bear with me here. In the 70's we had books with names such as the Population Bomb. It sold in the millions. The book was written by Dr. Paul R. Ehrlich, a Stanford biologist. In it he stated if we didn't practice birth control millions would starve and England would not exist in the year 2000. India was doomed and 65 million Americans would also starve. The population of the world was half what it is today and here we are. Are people starving? Yes, people are starving as a result of war and corruption, ethnic cleansing and manmade human ills. Most of which are/were caused by Globalists to further their agenda, for greed, control or both. We waste by some estimates 40% of the food here in America. How much food do we throw out? I'll admit it, more than I'd like. Think about all the front and back lawns all over America that grow grass instead of food. Think of all the water poured onto lawns. With that in mind how many people do you really think this earth could feed? This population scare of the 70's didn't work because people in first world countries cannot be made to panic with a full pantry and fridge. Something better was needed. Something that everyone on Earth could be made to be afraid of. The Globalists learned a long time ago that fear is a powerful tool for control. So what's Disney doing about it? Making blockbusters about the same thing. The Avengers movie Infinity Wars and Endgame are about a bad guy named Thanos, the movies have box office sales of over a 2 billion worldwide and counting. In the movies, Thanos is the most powerful being in the universe. He would sadly, and with a broken heart, have to go from planet to planet and kill half the population. If he did not eliminate half of each planets population they would all die because they would use up all the planets resources. Just like the population scare of the 70's and now climate change. This is what our children are being conditioned to believe. "Ah, come on, it's just a movie," you say. Yes, it's just a movie, but the message is there none the less. Let's not forget that when Hitler seized power in Germany he took complete control of the German movie industry as well as all radio stations. He also controlled what was taught in schools. The Globalists are coming at us from every conceivable angle. They've been doing this for 100 plus years. They are masters of deceit. Fear is how they wrested control from congress of our money with their creation of the United States Federal Reserve. Do these power mad, egotistical elites agree on everything, of course not?

When everyone in attendance thinks they walk on water there is bound to be conflict. Unfortunately they work those conflicts out on their insidious march towards a One World Government.

Chapter 2

The Federal Reserve

"Permit me to issue and control the money of a nation and I care not who makes its laws." Mayer Amschel Rothschild.

"And I sincerely believe with you, that banking institutions are more dangerous than standing armies; and that the principle of spending money to be paid by posterity, under the name of funding, is but swindling futurity on a large scale." Thomas Jefferson.

Some of the Globalist Families I've mentioned earlier control the creation of the dirty paper in your wallet. Let's find out how that privilege, so important to a strong economy and a free citizenry, was taken out of the hands of congress. The Constitution tells us in Article 1, section 8, "Congress shall have power...To borrow money, to coin money, regulate the value thereof, and of foreign coin, and fix the standards of weights and measures: and to provide for the punishment of counterfeiting...No state shall...coin money: emit bills of credit: or make anything but gold and silver coin a tender payment of debts. Congress is no longer in the money business. The result, disaster. Let's find out how that happened. While we're at it a think I can tell you why President Trump has a picture of Andrew Jackson in the Oval Office. So what did Jackson do, quite a lot? Enough to have an assassination attempt on his life. Again, unfortunately, we did not learn about his most important achievement in school. We have to go back to the past very briefly to understand the train wreck called the Federal Reserve, surreptitiously thrust upon the deceived American congress in December 1913. For this chapter I drew on many sources. The one thing all of the sources had in common was that the Federal Reserve was created in great secrecy. To be fair I researched a book by a cheerleader for the Federal Reserve called

America's Bank, by Roger Lowenstein. This book is endorsed on the back cover by two former heads of the Federal Reserve, Paul Volker and Ben Bernanke, it too states that the Fed was created and planned under utmost secrecy. The question that I hope springs to your mind is why the secrecy? If the Federal Reserve banking system was/is good for the American people why did the founders of the Federal Reserve hide like criminals? Here is the definition of conspiracy according to Oxford: a secret plan by a group to do something unlawful or harmful. We know from all sources that the first half of the definition of conspiracy regarding the creation of the Fed is true. As we read on you decide if the second half, the unlawful and harmful part, is fulfilled by the history of the Fed. The book by the cheerleader (Roger Lowenstein) did have an interesting quote in it from Nelson Aldrich, the powerful senator from Rhode Island, maternal grandfather of the Rockefeller Brothers and head of the Senate Finance Committee at the time, he said, "I grow sick with the thought that I am to remain one of that herd of dumb, driven cattle which makes up the mass of men." His grandsons and great grandsons feel the same way... about us.

In colonial days you had colonies printing their own money in an effort to be free of the Bank of England controlled by the Rothschilds. Massachusetts was the first to do it to finance its clashes with Quebec. The other colonies liked what they saw and did the same. Free money. There was no central government to regulate it. When more was needed it was simply printed. The money was not redeemable by gold or silver, thus it had no real value. This caused economic disaster in the colonies. Prices soared as a result of inflation. That last sentence is important as most people when asked what inflation is will say rising prices. That is not true. You hear the term inflation used incorrectly by economists all the time (the same ones that get their predictions wrong 50% of the time). Inflation is inflating the money supply. The more money that is pumped into an economy the less it is worth. When money is worth less it takes more of it to buy the same goods or services. Rising prices are the result of inflation. Rising prices are the result of printing more money. We've all heard of it taking 2 million Petros (the Venezuelan dollar) to buy a bag of flour. That's hyperinflation. This is from the late Professor of Economics, Antony Sutton. Antony was also a Research Fellow at the Hoover Institute on War, Revolution and Peace at Stanford University. Former congressman and presidential candidate Dr. Ron Paul agrees on the above true definition of inflation in his book: End the Fed.

When it became clear to the colonists that the money was worthless the colonists no longer wanted to accept it. This is where the term "not worth a colonial" came from. Laws had to be put in place to force people to use it. The whole situation became untenable and was finally sorted out after the Revolutionary War was won and the constitution was written in 1787. In article 1 section 8 in the preceding paragraph we see that the framers of the constitution were precise in their verbiage. It begins with "only congress", there is no room for interpretation. The framers knew how vitally important a nation's money supply was to prosperity and more importantly freedom.

Very early in The United States history, bankers wanted control of the money supply. They wanted the U. S. to have a central bank based on the European model the Rothschilds had put in place in numerous countries in Europe. Unfortunately they succeeded. The first Central Bank in what would become the United States began in 1782. The bank was called The Bank of North America. The Bank of North America was modeled on the Rothschild controlled Bank of England. The Bank of North America, as the Federal Reserve is today, was a private institution. As you can imagine, then as now people got rich. The Bank of North America did not survive the end of the Revolutionary War. The key take away here is: with the bank of North America fractional banking was introduced to the colonies. This meant that only a fraction of the total deposits in the bank had to be in the bank. The rest could be loaned out at interest. The problem with fractional banking is, what if everyone wanted their deposits at the same time? This would create a run on the banks. We saw this as a nation in the fall of 1930, 16 years after the Fed as we know it was sold to congress and the American people to prevent such economic upheavals. The second central bank, created after the revolutionary war was won was called the Bank of the United States. It was the first bank of that name. The driving force behind this bank was Alexander Hamilton. The person most notably against the bank was Jefferson. While Jefferson agreed that only congress should coin money, and print money backed by gold or silver, he did not feel that the constitution gave the federal government the power to create a central bank. In 1791 the bank was given a 20 year charter. Like the Bank of North America before it the Bank of the United States became a federal funds depository. At this time the bank had to back the paper money with gold or silver. This made it difficult or impossible to print money out of thin air. This second central bank of the U. S. was not all bad. Given the fact that it was ran by bankers that's quite a statement. The old saying, the first thing we do is get rid of the lawyers should be the first thing we do is get rid of the bankers. When the United States Bank's 20 year charter came up for renewal in 1811 the charter of the Bank of the United States was defeated in the senate by one vote, that of Vice-President George Clinton. In 1816 the second bank of the United States was chartered, again for a period of 20 years. It operated much like the first Bank of the United States, it allowed for private investors. Many historian agree that the Rothschilds were heavily invested in the second bank as well as the first Bank of the United States. At this time (four years after the war of 1812) the U. S. was in a boom cycle. The west was wide open and influential bankers wanted to invest there. At first the Bank of the United States demanded that any money lent to these other bankers would be paid back in real money, gold or silver. When the bankers, not part of the Bank of the United States demanded the same when they lent money, the Bank of the United States acquiesced. So now though the gold standard was in place the banks were corrupt and ignoring it. This corruption did not go unnoticed by President Andrew Jackson. In 1832 the Bank of the United States had only 4 years left on its charter. It was no secret that President Jackson loathed the bank and for that matter bankers, calling them a den of vipers. There were cartoons back then appearing in newspapers of Jackson with a sword in his hand attacking a hydra like creature with the many heads being those of well-known bankers. The chief head and the largest, appearing in a top hat, was that of Nicholas Biddle. Nicholas Biddle was the head of the second bank of the name, The Bank of The United States starting in 1822. By all accounts he was a brilliant man, and ruthless. Knowing that Jackson was coming up for reelection he requested that congress put the charter of the bank up for early renewal. He gambled that Jackson would not go all in against the bank and its powerful interests in an election year. Biddle was dead wrong. Jackson vetoed the charter of the second Bank of The United States. Two things happened after that. For the first and only time in the history of the United States, the nation had no national debt. All this without an income tax. The second thing that happened as a result of the banks veto was an assassination attempt on Jackson's life. This too was a first for the United States. On January 30, 1885 the first attempt on a president's life was made. Jackson was leaving the state capital after a funeral. Richard Lawrence was an unemployed painter from England. He pulled a pistol and fired at Jackson. The pistol misfired. He then pulled a second pistol, it too misfired. Here's the beautiful part. Instead of Jackson running or standing paralyzed with fright he took his walking stick and starts beating the tar out of Lawrence. Jackson was 67 at the time, ya gotta love this guy! After the assassination attempt the pistols that misfired were tested, they both worked perfectly. Some sources say they misfired because of the humid air, some say this misfired because of divine intervention. The would be assassin Richard Lawrence stated that with the president dead "money would be more plenty." He was shipped off to an insane asylum.[23] Jackson stated after the incident that it was his political enemies that wanted him dead. Then as now, would be assassins are either quickly killed as in the case of Lee Harvey Oswald, or shipped off never to be heard from again, as in the case of Lawrence. We have now arrived at the point in history of the current central bank of the United States called The Federal Reserve.

In the dark, on a winter night in November 1910, five men met surreptitiously at a train station in New Jersey. They boarded a train car with the name Aldrich on it. Having a train car in those days was like owning a jet airplane today. These were powerful men, and rich. The 5 men were Nelson Aldrich, Rhode Island Senator and head of the senate finance committee, maternal grandfather to the five Rockefeller brothers. Abraham Piatt Andrew, Ass. Secretary of the U. S. Treasury. Frank Vanderlip, president of The National City Bank of New York. National City Bank of New York was one of the most powerful banks at the time. It is currently known as Citibank under the corporate umbrella of Citigroup and was designated one of the banks "to big to fail" after the mortgage meltdown. Then as now it was and is a Rockefeller bank. Henry P. Davison, senior partner of the J. P Morgan Company. Paul Warburg, a partner in Kuhn, Loeb and Company. The two most important among the five were Paul Warburg and Nelson Aldrich. Paul Moritz Warburg August 10, 1869 – January 24, 1932, was a German born banker. The Warburg banking dynasty dated back to the late 1700's. He married into the Loeb family of Kuhn, Loeb and Company. He was made a director of Wells Fargo (also designated too big to fail after the mortgage meltdown) in 1910. He resigned that post to join the new Federal Reserve Board in 1914. He also had close ties to the Rothschild banking family. He was part of the five to guide the others as to how to create a central bank based on the European models established by the Rothschilds. He was also instrumental in the founding of the CFR in 1921. The five men were ostensibly on their way to Jekyll Island to go duck hunting. Jekyll Island is a private island off the coast of Georgia. The hunting lodge on the island, which was their destination, was completely cleared of guests by J. P Morgan

---

23   Robert Remini, *The Life of Andrew Jackson, New York, New York, Harper and Row Publishers inc.*

who owned the place. The fact that this meeting took place is not in question, nor is the fact that it was done in utmost secrecy. There is one more sad fact, we were never taught about it in public school. Like all things bad for the American public there had to be a reason to get the Federal Reserve act past the American people and congress. You can call the following events false flag events. The two events most directly attributed to the end run to create the Fed were the panic of 1883 and 1907. Then as today the Globalists have been masters of manipulation using their control of banks, industry, politicians and newspapers to further their agenda. In those days the agenda was greed driven. They wanted all the money.

The Panic of 1883 and 1907 conditioned the American people to fear economic upheavals/recessions. There was no welfare at the time. If you lost your job because of one of these created conditions you could likely starve, along with your family. These created conditions softened up the American psyche for a solution. The people that were behind the formation of the Fed were the very people that created the panics in the first place as Professor Carroll Quigley tells us on pages 71-73 of Tragedy and Hope. The Panic of 1907 resulted in the loss of half the stock markets value. These crises' and every other banking panic in the United States lead to greater centralization and thus less competition for the very powers that created the crises. As John D. Rockefeller was fond of saying "competition is a sin." This is a formula that is on perpetual repeat. It was J. P Morgan that literally bailed out the U. S. Government in the Panic of 1907. He made a handy profit doing so. This from the J. P Morgan website. It was his son that was also an early founder of the CFR. These panics need a couple key ingredients, money to steer markets and banks, and culpable politicians in the aftermath to help consolidate the power of the bankers as well as the government that the bankers control to an ever larger degree. The politician in the 1907 panics aftermath was none other than Nelson Aldrich. He established and chaired a commission to investigate the crisis. He also proposed a solution. This was part of the drive that led to the Creation of the Feral Reserve.

The mortgage meltdown of 2008 or 2009, as some say, is a good example of the consolidation of banking power, the elimination of the wrong banks and the gaining of even more power by the Federal Government. The true month and year of the mortgage meltdown was March, 2007. That is when the so called liar loans went away. The liar loans were referred to in the industry as stated income loans. It worked like this. Starting in 2001 if you had a 620 credit score (680 is a middle score, not good, not bad) you could get a home loan from the bank with 0 money down. Your loan would be called an 80/20 loan and look like this: 80% of the loan would be a first trust deed at about 6 to 8%. The remaining 20% of the loan would be a second trust deed at anywhere from 9.25% to 12% depending on credit. The 80% first loan was an interest only loan typically fixed for 2, 3, 5, or 7 years. The interest only aspect of the loan saved the borrower about $100 per $100,000 borrowed. There were two problems with this interest only feature, though it saved the borrower money because of the interest only aspect of the loan, no money was going to principle. The second problem was that after the initial 2, 3, 5 or 7 year fixed period, the loan would then reset for the remaining time on the first loan at an adjustable rate and be fully amortized. This meant that even had the new rate stayed the same after the 2,3,5,or 7 year period the payment would go up because of the full amortization (an additional $100 per every $100,000 borrowed) and the shorter amortization period. The adjusted first would now be fully amortized over 28, 27, 25 or 23 years, depending on how long it was fixed for in the initial contract. The shorter the amortization period the higher the payment. What's worse is these loans required no w2's, pay stubs or bank statements. Thus the name liar loans. As you can imagine people took advantage of these ridiculously "loose" guidelines and bought homes like they were candy nationwide. The ease by which these loans could be gotten created huge demand. The demand then caused the prices to go up literally 20% a year for 6 years, supply and demand. This was a true house of cards that came tumbling down at the expense of the American homeowner (former) and the American taxpayer. The homeowner lost his/her home and the American taxpayer got to bail out the banks under Obama. The banks got to make money on the high interest rate for the ridiculously risky loans they designed as well as the upfront bank fees. The banks then got to foreclose on the Americans who could no longer make their payments and claim a loss. As a nice ancillary benefit, a great deal of their competition failed or had to be bought up by the banks who survived for pennies on the dollar, with funds from the American taxpayer funded bailout. None of this could have happened without Wall Street buying these train wrecks, wrapping them in silk and then reselling them in the form of mortgage backed securities and various other financial instruments. The repercussions are still being felt in terms of an American buying a house today. An appraisal now costs $100 more because the government had to point the finger at someone other than the true criminals, so they created Appraisal Management Companies

(AMC's). These companies determine which appraiser does an appraisal randomly to be "fair." This keeps the seller or home flipper from colluding with the appraiser to bring the price in higher. The problems arise when an appraiser whose turn it is to do an appraiser comes from out of the area and doesn't know that though the houses look the same on the other side of this or that thoroughfare and it is the same city, the neighborhoods are quite different. One being far more desirable than the other. This is another example of the governments over reach making things worse for the consumer. The thinking was that appraisers had artificially inflated the value of houses so that real estate agents and or homes flippers/sellers could make more money. That premise is ridiculous as all mortgage banks have an appraisal review professionals in their bank whose job it is, is to go over each appraisal. On top of that if an appraiser brings in 3 appraisals in a calendar year whose value is not supported on the appraisal properly, they can lose their appraisal license. New educational requirements came out as well costing the loan officers approximately $350 per year. That cost and the higher appraisal cost will of course be borne by the perspective homeowner as she or he struggle to buy a home. On top of that the government decided to create a three day mandatory waiting period so that a borrower after 22 days or so in escrow would have time to make sure he/she still wanted to go forward with the purchase, another ridicules premise. So after saving for years, looking for a house for possibly months because some offers were not accepted, the government requires buyers to stop at the end and think about it for three dead days. This is very good for the banks. Instead of the borrower being able to lock his or her loan for 15 days because the market conditions are favorable (rates went down), he/she must lock on a 30 day because of the extra 3 days mandated by the government. A 30 day rate lock is .125 (1/8) higher than a 15 day lock. This is a huge boon for the banks. Think of the interest they make on that tiny .125% per say $500,000. On a per loan basis the math works out to an additional $37 a month or $444 a year for the bank. In 2018 there were approximately 5.96 million homes bought in the U. S. Let's take that $444 per year and multiply it by just 5 million homes. $444/5,000,000 =2,220,000,000, 2.2 billion extra a year, not bad. The two politicians most directly culpable were Rep Barney Frank and Senator Chris Dodd, a CFR member and Bilderberg member or attendee. The bill is known in the industry as Dodd/Frank, the full euphemistic name is "The Wall Street Reform and Consumer Protection Act." The bill was signed into law by Obama on 7-21-2010. How any banker in his/her right mind thought making a 100% loan to someone with below average credit score and no proof of ability to pay was a viable loan product defies logic. The meltdown was a planned event. Most people believe that the bank bailout was 700 billion. The Special Inspector General for TARP says the true amount was 16.8 trillion.[24]

Unfortunately that is not all, JP Morgan Chase, Wells Fargo, B of A, Citigroup, Morgan Stanley, Goldman Sachs Group, Inc. and Credit Suisse were all designated too big to fail as a result of the mortgage meltdown. Too big to fail means you can make whatever risky investments you want with depositors money, and if those investments fail, the American taxpayer is ready to bail you out with money printed out of thin air by the Fed. Ron Paul has a great quote regarding these government bailouts, he calls them privatized profits and socialized losses. Some of the banks here on the west coast that failed were Washington Mutual and Wachovia. All of the above led to the Great Recession. Like the great Depression, the Illuminated Ones made bank…pardon the pun.

So in 1910 we have five men surreptitiously meeting at Jekyll Island. As Ron Paul put it in his book End the Fed, the five men comprised two Morgan men, two Rockefeller men and one man, Paul Warburg, representing European banking interests most notably the Rothschilds, and quarterbacking the sordid affair. Now with the American public properly conditioned it was time to get a bill before congress. Given the egos involved there was some decent as to what the bill should be called. Nelson Aldrich got his way and the first failed bill was called the Aldrich Bill and was co-sponsored by Congressman Vreeland. The bill was never released from committee as it had Aldrich's name on it. At that time the American public was aware he was part of the Eastern Establishment. One thing the conspirators did agree on was that the new bank could not be called a Central Bank. These men knew that the American public and congress would have deep misgivings about the term central bank. Thus the name Federal Reserve. To further cover their tracks and create the appearance of the Fed not being a central bank they divided it up into 12 districts spread all over the nation. The real power resides in the New York branch with the other 11 kowtowing to the direction it takes, whatever direction that may be. The other problem the conspirators had was President Taft who won election in 1908 easily

24   https:www.google.com?amp/s/www.forbes.com/sites/mikecollins/2015/07/14/the-big-bank-bailout/amp.

and was looked upon as unbeatable in 1912. Taft at one time the darling of big business and bankers was showing signs of not going along. The democratic presumptive nominee was to be Wilson, a past president of Princeton University from 1902-1910. Wilson was a bit like Joe Biden, not the most dynamic of speakers. It was believed by the powers that be that Wilson could not beat Taft. Something had to be done to weaken Taft. The answer appeared in the form of former President Teddy Roosevelt. Taft was a Republican as was Teddy. In the election of 1912 Teddy created the Bull Moose Party. This new party split the Republican vote between Taft and Teddy, and voila, pro banking and malleable Wilson became president. There were newspapers controlled by the bankers and their allies that were painting Taft in a bad light while building up Wilson, just like what you see today. In December of 1913 with a large part of congress away for Christmas vacation, the bill managed to make it through both houses and was signed into law by Wilson on December 23, 1913. Congress had now lost the power to coin money. This is very important so I want to be as eloquent as I can regarding the Federal Reserve, It ain't federal and it ain't got no reserves! The Federal Reserve is a corporation. Government entities are never incorporated. The printing of money is now in private hands. It gets worse in that there is no congressional oversite. There have been congressmen over the years that have tried to create some kind of accountability regarding the Fed, all have failed. The congressmen that brought said bills to the floor got to watch them buried in committee. A quick word on how the dollar in your pocked used to look.

In the top left corner of your dollar bill it says: This note is legal tender for all debts public and private. This was not always the case. As late as 1931 it said the following: Redeemable in gold on demand at the United States Treasury or in gold or lawful money at any Federal Reserve Bank, (again, there are 12 Federal Reserve Bank branches in the United States, the most powerful of which is the New York branch). This meant that the Fed, as much as they would have liked to, could not create money out of thin air. For every "note" printed, there had to be a corresponding amount of gold available to redeem or make the note real. This made it impossible for the bankers to inflate the money supply and thus cause higher prices, among other things that we'll get to. You may think, how the U. S. government could have that much gold around when houses cost a $500,000, a million and more. The answer is simple, houses cost that much because the dollar is not backed by gold. A quick example: In 1976 in southern California a home that cost $40,000 now costs $625,000. That house bought in 1976 was 6 years after Nixon took the U. S. completely off the gold standard. The ability to inflate the money supply and the corresponding rise in prices are due to the dollar not being backed by gold or other hard currency such as silver. Prior to 1971 that same home would have sold for $23,000. These numbers I have used happen to be from my mother's home sales history. When you hear of the government giving a stimulus package to say the auto industry or the banking industry in the form of the 16 trillion dollar bailout discussed earlier, have you wondered what that does to the dollar in your pocket, or the hard earned money you put in the bank. It makes those dollars' worth less. It is what G. Edward Griffin in his brilliant book, The Creature from Jekyll Island, calls an invisible tax. This is the primary reason prices always go up. A quick internet search will tell you that the United States national debt is 23 to 25 trillion depending on the source. I believe it to be at least triple that amount. It's hard to say because of the Fed's lack of oversite and their arcane accounting practices. Let's take just a 20 trillion dollar debt and do some simple math to determine what we pay in interest on a monthly and yearly basis. Let's use 3% interest to err on the low side. 20,000,000,000,000/3%= $600,000,000,000 per year and $50,000,000,000 per month. The equation above is interest only. The monthly payment does not hit any of the principle. That is 600 billion a year and 50 billion a month paid to whom? The families of the people mentioned at the beginning of this chapter that created the Fed. You may be thinking that China and other countries own some of the U. S. debt, which is true. Just like we own some of their debt. The reality is that the United States through the IMF (International Monetary Fund), the World Bank, and the BIS (Bank of International Settlements), loans more money than any other nation in the world. All of this made possible by the taxes you pay as an American citizen. This all ties into the caravans at the southern border. First let's see how the cartel conjure money out of air.

This next concept was difficult for me to grasp. Money is created out of thin air by debt… What?? Thanks to G. Edward Griffin, it finally made sense to me. That and a little help from Marriner Eccles the governor of the Fed in 1941. On page 187-188 of The Creature from Jekyll Island, Griffin supplies us with the following. Modern monetary systems have a fiat base-literally money by decree-with depositary institutions, acting as fiduciaries, creating obligations against themselves with the fiat base acting in part as reserves. The decree appears on the currency notes: This note is legal tender for all debts, public and private." While no individual could refuse to accept such money for debt repayment, exchange contracts could easily be made to thwart its use in everyday commerce. However, a forceful explanation as to why money is accepted is that the federal government requires it for the payment of tax liabilities. Anticipation of the need to clear this debt creates a demand for the pure fiat dollar.[25] On September 30, 1941 Eccles was asked to give testimony before the House Committee on Banking and Currency. The purpose of the hearing was to obtain information regarding the role of the Federal Reserve in creating conditions that lead to the depression of the 1930's. Congressman Wright Patman, was the Chairman of the committee. He asked the Governor how the Fed got the money to purchase two billion dollars' worth of government bonds in 1933.That 2 billion in 1933 dollars is at least 40 billion in today's money. Here is the following exchange.

Eccles: We created it.

Patman: Out of what?

Eccles: Out of the right to issue credit money.

Patman: And there is nothing behind it, is there, except our governments credit?

Eccles: That is what our money system is. If there were no debts in our money system, there wouldn't be any money.

This is "one" of the ways the Federal Reserve creates money. This money is a debt with interest attached…you pay the interest. One of the primary reasons we have caravans immigrating to this country is the banking system we have in place and government corruption.

When a South American nation has resources that well connected billionaires in our country wish to exploit and our government gets an ancillary benefit like control of that countries dictator and thus control of the country, several things happen. Dark forces in the CIA or NSA determine a likely candidate to run the country. In the case of Iran it was the Shah, the resource,

---

25   *"Money, Credit and Velocity," Review, May, 1982, Vol. 64, No. 5, Federal Reserve Bank of St. Louis,* p. 25.

oil. In South American countries it could be oil, timber, fruit, believe it or not, and minerals. As we read in chapter one of this book the Shah was just one example of powerful private forces wanting to pillage a nation of its resources. It works like this according to John Perkin's fascinating autobiographical book, Confessions of an Economic Hit Man. Leaders of undeveloped countries are approached to take substantial loans for large construction projects to develop their natural resources. The hook for the loan is the companies cutting the trees, mining the minerals or extracting the oil must be American. The other hook is the leader and his family will be rich. The poor will of course suffer. If they are tribal and in the way they'll be moved off land their ancestors roamed for centuries. Perkins goes on to say that at times force is needed. He calls the men that apply the force Jackals. They do the wet work. Wet being blood. In his book he describes attempts on Hugo Chavez's life. Hugo was not playing ball. So when you look at the caravans from El Salvador, Guatemala and Honduras keep in mind that CFR member presidents and their cabinets are culpable along with the foreign leaders of the various countries themselves. The swamp has tentacles that reach all over the world. This is the mess they've left for President Trump. The loans are administered by the IMF or the World Bank mentioned in the first chapter. Both of these entities are creatures of the United States Federal Reserve. They would not exist without the U. S. dollar. These loans are wrapped in the euphemistic term international aid. The IMF term is Structural-Adjustment Loans.

Corrupt Minister of Finance and dictatorial presidents from Asia, Africa and Latin America are tripping over their own expensive footwear in their unseemly haste to "get adjusted." For such people money has never been easier to obtain then it is today; with no complicated projects to administer and no messy accounts to keep, the venal, the cruel and the ugly are laughing literally all the way to the bank. For them structural adjustment is like a dream come true. No sacrifices are demanded of them personally. All they have to do –amazing but true,-is screw the poor, and they've already had plenty of practice at that. Griffin, p.101-102.[26] These dictators then live a lavish life style partying like rock stars as the people suffer. When the money runs out they get another loan to pay the interest on the first loan, thus becoming perpetual servants to the Globalists. All of this made possible by the Fed.

---

26   Graham Hancock, Lords of Poverty: The Power, Prestige, and corruption of the International Aid Business (New York: Atlantic Monthly Press, 1989) pp.59, 60.

Where the World Bank go's (ran by men such as Robert McNamara who lied to get the U. S. into war in Vietnam) disaster follows. The disaster is called socialism. From Africa to Asia to South America the result is the same. President Trump keeps pointing to Venezuela in an attempt to convince Americans that socialism is a train wreck. Venezuela is simply the latest example. I quick word on the International Monetary Fund and the World Bank.

Both the IMF and the World Bank were created in 1944 in Bretton Woods New Hampshire. You should think of them as the children the Fed doesn't want to talk about. They are both headquartered in Washington D. C. The presidents of the World Bank have always been Americans up until 2012 when a naturalized American citizen, Jim Yong Kim became president. He was the former Chair of the Department of Global health and Social Medicine at Harvard and a past president of Dartmouth, excellent Globalist pedigree. The head of the IMF though headquartered in D. C. has always been a European. Here is a look at the Presidents of the World Bank and their interconnectedness to the Globalists and their machinations mentioned in the first chapter.

Eugene Meyer: President 1946-1946. He's family owned and controlled the Washington post for all of the 20th century until they sold to Bezos. He was also a chairman of the Fed.

John McCloy: 1947-1949, we spoke of him on chapter one, he had no banking experience before becoming World bank President. Chairman of the CFR from 1953-1970. He was succeeded by one of the boys he taught to sail, David Rockefeller, who was Chairman Emeritus until his demise in 2017.

Eugene Black: 1949-1963, former Chase Bank Executive before the merger with Morgan.

George Woods: 1963-1968, former V. P. of Chase Bank.

Robert McNamara: 1968-1981, mentioned earlier, no prior banking experience. CFR member.

Aiden Clausen: 1981-1986, Former executive at Bank of America.

Barber Conable: 1986-1991, Former U. S. State Senator, no previous banking experience.

Lewis Preston: 1991-1995, former bank executive of J. P Morgan, CFR member.

James Wolfensohn: Former business partner of past Federal Reserve Chairman Paul Volker, deep Eastern Establishment ties, CFR member.

Paul Wolfowitz: 2005-2007, Chief architect of the Iraq invasion of 2003. He had to resign as president of the World Bank due to an ethics scandal. No previous banking experience. CFR member.

Robert Zoellick: 2007-2012, deep establishment ties in both the public and private sectors. Deep ties with the Bush's. He was George H. W.'s Deputy Chief of Staff among many other public posts including Executive vice President and General Counsel of Fannie Mae. In 2005 he was George W's. Deputy Secretary of State. We could write a book about this guy alone. Of particular interest is the fact that as of 2018 he became a Twitter board member. In light of Twitter's censorship of what are called right wing views this is no surprise. CFR member.

Jim Yong Kim: 2012-2019, discussed earlier.

All Presidents of the World Bank have an additional common thread. They are all either Bilderberg Members or were/are frequent attendees.

Ostensibly the World Bank and the IMF create loans to help impoverished third world nations. A brief conversation with a member of any of dozens of environmental or human rights groups would quickly and passionately but an end to that bit of fiction. One of the more devastating impacts of the World Bank and IMF is the funding of Dams from Asia to Africa and South America. The environmental impact is absolutely horrendous. Dams are great for the dictator or totalitarian government getting the funding from the IMF or World Bank, for the people downstream…not so much. These are the already poor or lower middle class people struggling to eke out a living. If you're a fishermen your entire stream of income and those of you village's economy is gone. This is a scenario played out all over the world for decades. In some cases the dams built to ostensibly provide cheap electrical power have the price of that power inflated by corrupt government officials to make the almighty Indian Rupee, the Brazilian Real, or the Venezuelan Bolivar, or whatever that third world nation's monetary unit is called. Here are a few examples from several decades.

50 years ago two Mega dams were funded by the World Bank and built in the Democratic Republic of Congo. The communities displaced by the Inga and Kariba dams are still fighting for compensation and economic rehabilitation. The dam did provide electricity to the less than 10% of the Congolese people that use electricity. Meanwhile not only were the people displaced but the dam's diversion of fresh water caused species extinction.[27] Over the last 50 years the World Bank and the IMF have been busy. In India, the World Bank funded the construction of a dam that displaced 2 million people, flooded 360 square miles, and wiped out 81,000 acres of forest cover. In Brazil, it spent a billion dollars to "develop" a part of the Amazonian basin and to fund a series of hydroelectric projects. It resulted in deforestation of an area half the size of Great Britain and has caused great human suffering because of resettlement. In Kenya, the Bura irrigation scheme caused such desolation that a fifth of the population abandoned the land. The cost was $50,000 per family served.

Livestock projects in Botswana led to the destruction of grazing land and the death of thousands of migratory animals. This resulted in the inability of the natives to obtain food by hunting, forcing them into dependence on the government for survival. Griffin p. 102. Based on the track record of the World Bank/IMF their goal is not the betterment of mankind. Their goal is to strengthen their grip on petty dictators that control the people while they control the dictators. If that is not the case then the presidents of the World Bank and the IMF must be the most monumentally stupid people on the planet.

As stated earlier, when money is loaned out the boys at the Fed don't go and open the vault and take reserves out, there aren't any. They print the money. That is inflation which causes the money you worked for to be worth incrementally less. This is going on all over the world including here in our own country where it is called bailouts.

---

27   *The Guardian. Bringing back big bad dams, by Peter Bosshard.*

The Bank of International Settlements (BIS) is owned by the Central Banks of various countries. It was founded in 1930 and is headquartered in Basel Switzerland. The U. S., Belgium, France, Germany, the United Kingdom, Japan and Switzerland were founding members. In the last chapter we spoke of international bankers providing funding for countries to fight wars. It is interesting that the three Axis nations of Germany, Italy and Japan were all founding members, as well as their chief enemies (in WW2) the U. S., the U. K. and France were also founding members. An interesting tidbit about the BIS is that during the years between 1933 and 1945 BIS board members include Walther Funk a prominent Nazi, and Emil Puhl responsible for processing dental gold looted from concentration camp victims, as well as Hermann Schmitz, the director of IG Farben, and Baron von Schroeder, the owner of the J. H. Stein Bank.[28] Regarding IG Farben a book could be written about that company as well. IG Farben during WW2 relied on slave labor with as many as 30,000 coming from the camp at Auschwitz. One of Farben's subsidiaries made Zyklon B, the gas that killed millions in the Nazi gas chambers.

The subject of the Fed, the World Bank, the IMF and the BIS are worthy of an entire book. Some excellent ones have been written. The Creature from Jekyll Island by G. Edward Griffin is my favorite. It's a bit daunting at nearly 600 pages but so worth it. It's entertaining as well as informative. Ron Paul's: End the Fed is good but condensed at only a few hundred pages. Professor Antony Sutton's book: The Federal Reserve Conspiracy is only about 100 pages but is packed with info. It is difficult to find (I had to send off to San Francisco) but well worth it.

The Federal Reserve was created to end economic upheavals, recessions and depressions. A mere 14 years after the Feds inception we had the greatest depression our nation has ever known. It was followed by never ending boom and bust cycles the last of which was just a decade ago called the great recession. The Fed has failed miserably in its stated goal, economic stability. This is no accident. We need to end the Fed. The free market will in and of its self-determine interest rates based on the oldest economic law, supply and demand. Think of what this nation could do for our own people and other countries without the corrupt Federal Reserve.

---

28   Higham, Charles. Trading with the Enemy: The Nazi-American Money Plot, 1933-1949.

Chapter Three

President Trump and Climate Change

President Trump has been accused constantly, ad nauseam, of being a climate change denier. It is interesting to me that if you say, "I'm not sure mankind is causing it," you are a climate change denier. I'm also curious as to what happened to good old fashioned Global Warming? Why did the narrative change from Global Warming to Climate change? I'm writing about climate change in chapter three because the Globalist media is bombarding us with it with every tentacle they have, and they have a lot. They can't run against President Trump on his record so they have to paint him as a climate change denier, thus scaring the hell out of everyone with the constant media blitz of, "It's an existential threat," repeated by the Democrats like a Voodoo chant. Everyone knows and agrees that climate changes. The question is what is the cause? Regarding a true environmental threat to this world, we'll get to that at the end of this chapter. There is a manmade threat and you never hear about it in the Globalist controlled news.

Before we begin let's not connect Global Warming with pollution. We are not talking about pollution. So you know where I'm coming from, I care about this planet as much or more than the next person. I had a deep appreciation of nature instilled in me as a kid. I never use plastic water bottles. The great Pacific garbage patch is a concern of mine. There are actually two of the patches, one between Hawaii and California and one between Hawaii and Japan. Theses garbage patches are mostly made of plastic. How many plastic water bottle do you think are in those "patches?" Like a lot of people I try not to use plastic bags if possible. I saw the video of the turtle with the straw in its nose. I was straw free decades before that video surfaced. So again, we are not talking about pollution we are talking about climate change.

In 2006 Al Gore came out with the documentary, An Inconvenient truth. I thought that movie was the best thing since sliced bread. It was so well presented. He had a huge graph showing rising temps in the last few decades where he had to get up on a ladder because the temps went so high on the graph. Great theatrics! I talked to anyone who would listen about it, "ya gotta see it", I said! I told people National Geographic was dedicating a whole Issue to it. I said that I would loan them that issue if they promised to give it back so I could loan it out again. National Geographic also said that they would continue to track Global Warming on a monthly bases. I can hear myself saying, "The Polar Bears are drowning because the ice melting and they're champion swimmers." I was Passionate about man made global warming, the newly converted to an ideology usually are. I was wrong. In my defense, if Big Oil was saying it was not caused by the burning of fossil fuels in the atmosphere you know they are lying! I thought of course they're going to say that, they put it there. The Globalists have done a masterful job of deception on the American people. First they had scientists from Big Oil deny man's effect on warming. This caused people like myself and millions of others to say, "It's gotta be true if those damn Globalists are denting it." The headlines then where along the lines of, scientists say earths warming do to the burning of fossil fuels, Big Oil denies. Then Big oil scientists (different than the first scientists) came out and said yes, it is fossil fuels. Ah ha, we knew it all of the time! We knew they were lying. So why would the masters of the universe potentially kill a cash cow such as oil? Two reasons. They have no intention of doing so. They can always command their media sycophants to report on other factors that "truly" caused climate change. Truth is a moving target with these people. Secondly they no longer need, care, or even want to count more billions. The previous chapter explains their grip on your wallet. They have a ton of money from their various central banks. The end came is control. The best way to control a world is a common enemy. The enemy, climate change. The control mechanism, a global carbon tax and the death of industry and economic expansion. Think of what a few months of the Coronavirus lockdown did to our economy. We've had a two trillion dollar government giveaway. We know that that money was printed out of thin air. In terms of a carbon tax killing industry there would be no phased reopening of the economy. The jobs would not be back. You would grovel at the feet of government for food. You would do whatever you were told so that your children would not starve. Your internet use would be tracked to make sure you were not visiting wrong thinking sites. In the latter stages of this scenario you would not get your ration of food because you looked on an improper site. Finally the herd would need to be culled because due to the existential threat of climate change we can't pump CO2 into the atmosphere from farming tractors to feed people. We can't have planes delivering the food to third world countries because of the risk to the climate. So as usual, third world nations will be hit first and hardest. If this scenario sounds whack to you it has already been proposed in congress by the nutjob congresswoman from New York, it's called the green new deal. We also had a Democratic Presidential Candidate like Tom Steyer, saying on his first day in office he would declare a climate emergency. Let's see what science has to say about all this. I'll also ask you to apply some common sense and a little critical thinking along the way.

A few facts to keep in mind.

When we exhale we are exhaling CO2. That's everyone on the planet, 7 .5 billion or so, and all the lions and tigers and bears. If there are too many of us breathing that could be construed as a problem. The solution seems simple to the Globalists, Population control. Yes, that is on their agenda. They feel they must cull the herd. You and I are the herd.

The majority of our oxygen comes from the ocean, not the rainforests, this from the Smithsonian Institution.

Oil does not come from dinosaurs. Any quick internet search will tell you that, from every source that pops up, yet it is taught in our schools...Why?

Oil comes from the rapid burial of dead microorganisms in environments where oxygen is scarce. This enables them to maintain their hydrogen-carbon bonds according to Scientific American.

NASA tells us the rotation of the earth is slowing.

Magnetic North is moving about 30 miles a year since the turn of this century.

NASA also tells us the sun has periods of high energy and low energy. Periods of more heat and less heat generated by the sun.

According to Danish Geophysicist Mads Faurschou Knudsen of the geology department of Aarhus University, Denmark and Peter Riisager of the Geological Survey of Denmark and Greenland (and Many others) The Earth's Magnetic field impacts climate. Let's keep all this in mind as we speak about "science". Shouldn't we consider that huge yellow/red thingy in the sky when we're talking about heat? Hmm, seems pretty straight forward to me. What about the Earth's Magnetic field? Our kids are not being taught any of those obvious possibilities. They are certainly not hearing it on the fake news.

In an article in the Telegraph by Sally Peck, we learn of a British High Court ruling concerning Al Gore's movie An Inconvenient Truth. If a teacher in the UK wishes to show the movie it must be accompanied by guidance notes. The notes are required because the film contains nine key errors. The nine errors are as follows.

Sea level rises in the immediate future of 7 meters. The film came out 14 years ago.

Low lying Pacific atolls are being inundated because of anthropogenic global warming.

The shutting down of the ocean conveyer. (had that happened we'd all be gone).

Rising CO2 could not be directly correlated to higher temps based on the two graphs Gore supplied.

Gore says that the disappearance of snow on Kilimanjaro was directly attributable to global warming. The judge said scientists have not established that the recession of snow on Kilimanjaro is primarily attributable to human induced climate change.

The film contends that Lake Chad is a prime example of global warming but the judge said there was insufficient evidence, and that " it is apparently considered to be far more likely to result from other factors, such as population increase and over grazing, and reginal climate variability".

Gore blames Hurricane Katrina and the consequent devastation in New Orleans on global warming, but the judge ruled insufficient evidence.

Gore said, "The Polar Bears are drowning." The judge said: The only science that either side before me can find is that four Polar Bears have recently been found drowned because of a storm.

Gore states that coral reefs all over the world were being bleached as a result of Global warming. The judge ruled that the stress could be over fishing or pollution.

Remember the film was made in 2006. Paramount, the film's distributer warns in a synopsis of the film that the vast majority of the world's scientists are right, we have just ten years to avert a major catastrophe. That was 14 years ago. I'm hearing from a true scientist, the freshman congress woman from New York that we now have 12 years left. I'm hearing from the majority of the Democrats running for president that Climate Change is an existential threat. What else are they going to come at President Trump with? The stock market that is securing the voters retirement, the one that continues to break record after record? I am seeing kids marching and having real animus towards President Trump because they are being brain washed that he's an existential threat to their future.

Let's talk about the sun. It seems to me that the source of all heat should be addressed. Is it not mind boggling to you that the suns energy output or lack thereof is never mentioned in the Globalist media's constant man made climate change indoctrination? Could it be that the sun has cycles of low and high energy (heat) output? Of course. Let's apply a little common sense. Then let's talk science.

The Earth was in a mini ice age circa 1415 to 1830. With a little effort you can pull up pictures of the Thames River in England frozen over. Millions starved worldwide because crops need sun to grow.

And the earth in many places was simply to cold. We have historical evidence of this Mini ice Age. Is it not logical to believe that if the sun goes into cooling phases that it goes into warming phases as well, such as the early 1990's? Pretty simple stuff right? What do scientists have to say about it?

In a 2017 article Dr. Gabriel Cousens tells us the following. In the first 6 months of 2017, 58 peer reviewed articles were published clearly indicating that we're no longer in a global warming cycle. The article goes on to state a direct correlation between sun spot activity and the suns energy output. More sunspots, more energy from the sun, equals a hotter Earth. Dr. Cousens relates that according to historical observation, it appears that Industrial Age manmade C02, on which the "Gore" theory is based has a negligible impact on both global warming and global cooling cycles. It is also clear that Gore's theory has not come true.

Nasa scientist John L. Casey has this to say about the sun in his excellent book Dark Winter. In the book he develops a descriptive theory on what he calls Relational Cycle (RC). RC theory postulate that geologic manifestations on Earth are the result of solar changes and sunspots. The theory has been about 90% accurate, in contrast to Al Gore's theory which has been consistently disproven. Casey goes on to tell us that the most reliable source for climate change prediction is the number of sunspots varying in 206 year sun cycles. Again, more sunspots more heat. Casey goes on to show graph after graph proving a direct correlation between sunspot activity and heat on this planet over centuries. He believes beginning around 2019 that we are entering a period of global cooling. As of November 2019 hundreds of cold records were shattered in the contiguous United States. That's November, before the winter of 2019/20 has begun. The same record colds were observable in the United States in the winter of 2018/19.

Here is an article that appeared in elctroverse.net, titled Professor Valentina Zharkova Breaks Her Silence and Confirms "Super" Grand Solar Minimum. The article is dated November 6, 2018. Valentina Zharkova Is a professor of Mathematics at Northumbria University. She has a BSc/MSc in applied Mathematics and Astronomy, a PH.D in Astrophysics and is a certified project manager. Here is the article in its entirety. Professor Valentina Zharkova gave a presentation of her Climate and the Solar Magnetic Field hypothesis at the Global Warming Policy Foundation in October, 2018. The information she unveiled should shake/wake you up. Zharkova was one of only two scientists to correctly predict solar cycle 24 would be weaker than cycle 23- in fact, only 2 out of 150 models predicted this. Zharkova's models have run at 97% accuracy and now suggest a Super Grand Solar Minimum is on the cards beginning in 2020. Grand Solar Minimums are prolonged periods of reduced solar activity, and in the past have gone hand in hand with times of global cooling. The last time we had a GSM (the Maunder Minimum) only two magnetic fields of the sun went out of phase. This time all four magnetic fields are going out of phase. If the world was looking for an epiphany moment, this should be it. Even if you believe the IPCC's worst case scenario, Zharkova's analysis blows any "warming" out of the water. There is a video attached to the above article. It is 17 minutes in duration and starts a bit slowly, still, it is well worth your time. In the video portion it is revealed that Professor Zharkova said this cooling would begin in about 2015 and by 2020 as stated above we would be in the Super Grand Solar Minimum. According to the next chapter directly below, she was right.

In Investor's Business daily we find this article titled "Don't Tell Anyone but we Just Had two Year of Record Breaking Cold." The article is dated 5-16-2018. Writing in Real Clear Markets, Aaron Brown looked at the official NASA global temperature data and noticed something surprising. From February 2016 to February 2018 global temperature dropped by an average of 0.56 degrees Celsius. That is the biggest two year drop in the past century. This fact got no mention in the fake media. Here's an article by James Murphy in The New American dated March, 2019 titled, An Inconvenient Glacier: Study shows Greenland Glacier Growing. Over the past two decades, the Jakobshavn Glacier in Greenland has been melting at what alarmists might call an alarming rate. However, a new study published in Nature Geoscience has concluded that since 2016 the Glacier has been growing. The satellite imagery used to determine this fact was from NASA's, Oceans Melting Greenland. The study was conducted by NASA's Jet Propulsion Laboratory. The jakobshavn Glacier was discharging the most ice in the Northern Hemisphere. For all of Greenland it is king. That discharge stopped in 2016.

In an article by Vijay Jayaraj (M.Sc., Environmental Science, University of East Anglia, England), in American Thinker dated March 14,2019. Vijay states that our main stream media has conveniently ignored for decades the role of the sun in determining Earth's climate. His fear is not global warming but global cooling. Think about it. Cops grow slower or not at all if there is not sufficient solar energy. He says that the repeated one-dimensional doomsday cry about carbon Dioxides role in global temperature blinds the public to other causes. He then states there is poor correlation between CO2 emissions and global temperature. He then goes on to site NASA and the role of sunspots. He then states that hundreds of scientific papers affirm the suns overwhelming impact on Earths temperature. I don't know about you but this seems very basic to me. There are hundreds of scientists adhering to the science of Global Cooling. They are saying to the alarmist scientists, "Here's our science, show us yours." The Globalist Media is lying to us…again. Here's an article from Newsweek, hardly a right wing climate denial magazine by Kristen Hugo dated 6/27/2018 titled: Volcanic Activity is Melting This Glacier From Below. The article states that the Pine Island Glacier is melting. Surprisingly, it's not climate change alone that is causing the thaw. New research by the national Science Foundation has found evidence that volcanic activity beneath the glacier is a likely culprit. An international team of scientists from NSF and the UK's Natural Environmental Research Council discovered an underwater heat source by tracing the chemical signature of helium underwater. The heat source is almost certainly in the form of underwater volcanic activity. The Pine Island Glacier is in the Western Antarctic. According to an article in Scientific American dated 7/6/2017 the East Antarctic Glaciers are growing. In an article about warm Antarctic caves, some of which are 70 degrees Fahrenheit there is a whole ecosystem of flora and fauna deep beneath the frozen surface. A study led by the Australian National University around Mount Erebus, an active volcano on Ross Island in Antarctica, showed extensive cave systems. In the caves they say you can wear a t-shirt. The article goes on to say that these caves are because of volcanos under the ice. There are 15 known volcanos with more being discovered all the time. Here's an article from the Smithsonian titled: The Mystery of an Underwater Volcano, by Danielle Hall. It states that three thousand feet below the surface in the middle of the Pacific Ocean, lies one of the world's largest volcanos, called Havre. The article goes on to state that it erupted for up to 90 days in 2012. The interesting thing is that it would not have been noticed had a passenger in a plane not seen and reported an oddly colored patch in the ocean. It was the largest deep water eruption in modern times and the only reason we know about it is because someone looked out a plane window at the right time and said something. Scientists estimate that it was as large as Mt. St. Helens. The article goes on to say that 70% of all volcanic eruptions happen beneath the surface of the ocean.

Here's an article from The Washington Post dated January 10, 2020, titled, It was an Enormous Underwater Volcano. Let's keep in mind that the Washington Post is far from a right wing publication, in other words the paper pushes the manmade climate change, pseudo-science. The article states that a huge underwater volcano was born circa June or July 2018 off the coast of Madagascar. They say it is one of the deepest magma chambers ever discovered, approximately 16 to 19 miles deep. Eleonora Rivalta, a physicist who studies earthquakes and volcanos at the German Research Center for Geosciences said once you create a channel to the surface, the magma starts to poor out and create a volcano. As you can imagine scientists from all over the world are studying this new phenomena. One scientist said a unique aspect of these studies show how quickly the magma can rise and create either a new volcano or an eruption. The paper goes on to say that "the amount of magma that moved might have been the greatest ever observed". So we've got underwater volcanos being discovered everywhere, popping up in some cases in a matter of months, and recently, yet we never hear that this does/could have an effect on ocean temperatures. This is basic, volcanos are hot. What if for the last 50 to 70 years there has been more underwater volcanic activity we simply did not know about. Here is yet another example of the gross oversimplification of manmade climate change alarmists. While writing this chapter one of my friends (a very intelligent attorney, yes they do exist) told me I was a misinformed climate change denier and that the oceans are now warmer than they have ever been. He went on to say that scientists have been tracking ocean temperatures for 50 years. I shot him over a few of the above articles. He didn't have a whole lot to say after that. I think this next article is powerful, it comes from The New American by Alex Newman dated Febuary, 2019. The title is: UN Scientist Blows the Whistle on Lies about Climate, Sea Level.[29] The United Nations Intergovernmental Panel on Climate Change (UN IPCC) is misleading humanity about climate change and sea levels, a leading expert on sea levels who served on the UN IPCC told The New American. In Fact, it is more likely that sea levels will decline, not rise, explained DR. Nils-Axel Morner, the retired head of the paleo geophysics and geodynamics at Stockholm University. A new solar-driven cooling period is not far off, he said. But when Morner tried to warn the IPCC that it was publishing false information that would inevitably be discredited, they simply ignored him. And so, he resigned in disgust and decided to blow the whistle. Asked if global cities such as Miami would be flooded due to sea level rise caused by alleged global warming, Moerner was unequivocal "Absolutely Not." "There is no rapid sea level rise and there will not be," he said, citing observable data. "On the contrary, if anything

---

29   http://WWW.thenewamerican.com/tech/environment/item/31472-un-ipcc-scientist-blow-whistle-on-un-climate-lies.

happens, the sea will go down a little." The widely respected scientist who has been tracking sea levels for 50 years, blasted those who use incorrect, "correlation factors" in their data to make it appear that sea levels are rising worldwide. That is just wrong he said. Indeed even speaking of something called "global sea level" is highly misleading, the expert explained. "It is different in different parts of the world." Morner said, noting that sea levels rise in one part of the world and decline in another depending on a variety of factors. For instance, the interview took place next to an 18th century Baltic Sea level marker in Saltsjobaden near Stockholm that showed the Baltic Sea level at the time it was made. Because the ground is rising, the marker is now higher up from sea level then when it was made. Morner has personally been measuring and tracking sea levels in equatorial regions of the world-Bangladesh, the Maldives, Southern India, New Caledonia, Fiji, and beyond. Mourner's conclusion is that solar activity and its effects on have been the dominant factor in what happens to both the climate and the seas. Meanwhile, the UN claims the current changes in climate and sea levels are attributable to human emissions of carbon dioxide (C02). Mankind's emissions of this essential gas, required by plants and exhaled by people, makes up a fraction of one percent of all so called greenhouse gases present naturally in the atmosphere. "Absolutaly not."Morner said about the C02 argument. Noting there was "something basically sick" in the blame C02 hypthosis. "C02, if it has any effect, it is minute- it does not matter. What has a big effect is the sun. Obviously, while he was serving on the UN IPCC, Morner tried to warn his colleagues on the UN body about the politically backed hypothesis about CO2 driving temperature change and the subsequent change regarding sea level rise were totally incorrect. "They just ignored what I was saying," he recounted. "If they were clever, if they had facts on their hands, they could show that "no, you're wrong." But this is not the case. They just will not discuss it. I will try to discuss it. I will show with their own data they are wrong. Because in science, we discuss. We don't forbid or neglect.

When asked about the frequently repeated (and easily debunked) claims of an alleged 97 percent consensus supporting the man made global warming hypothesis, Morner said it was simply not true- and even if it were, it would be irrelevant. "Why does anybody care about something when it is not correct," he asked. "They say it because they have applied excellent lobbyists. They are working with lobbyists in their hand; say this, do that. "We don't do that." In the field of physics Morner estimated that 80 to 90 percent of physicists know the hypothesis is wrong. "They claim there are 97 percent who are for it," Morner said. "I claim that it is 97 percent of scientific facts against them." Quoting Galileo, the 80 year old Swedish scientist also slammed the shady tactics used by climate alarmists and the lobbyists they work with to suppress the real facts and demonize those that contradict their alarmist narrative. "If you were to write an excellent paper in a peer-reviewed journal, but they didn't like it, they write to the journal and say they can't write things like that, it's against the general consensus." said Morner, who has published hundreds of peer reviewed papers on a wide range of scientific subjects. "They even put these journals on a black list." This is a shady thing going on. We don't work like that in real science.

Instead of science Morner suspects that the behind the scenes promoters of the manmade warming hypothesis have dark, ulterior motives. "I think the ultimate thing is that they want a government for the whole globe, and that is a weird idea," Morner said, criticizing the Rockefeller dynasty and global efforts to keep developing countries from developing under the guise of saving the climate. "This is the hope of controlling everything. It is autocracy. It is really bad. Nobody should rule like that. Authors note, this guy sounds like me...and many others. Back to the article, we are going to fast forward a bit. Speaking of the UN's "climate process." Morner was pleased with President Trump's actions so far, which include announcing that the US government would be withdrawing from the highly controversial UN Paris Agreement. He urged the Trump administration to "forget about" the whole UN climate agenda "because that is nonsense, and you very carefully and cleverly understood that." However, he also urged Trump to be empathetic and willing to discuss the climate issue. "It is very simple for us to discuss it, because we really have the facts, and they have their models," Morner said. "And facts are better than models." Author's note, this is the second highly regarded scientist in this text alone, saying to manmade climate change scientists, Show me your science, here is mine." Back to the article, because Morner is so spot on. "Of course everybody wants to believe in something," he said. "All of these people who don't know what they are talking about, but they want to save the world. "We don't change the world." The world will keep on going. "It is even worse than that though. "This is the most dangerous and frightening part of it: How such a lobbyist group has been able to fool the world," he concluded, comparing it to how national Socialists in Germany and communists in Russia and China were able deceive populations and seize power. Blasting the "autocratic process,' he said these organizations and deceitful forces were "so dangerous." He also expressed shock that the UN and governments would parade children at the UN summits. "What do they know? "They are very nice all of them, but they should be out playing, not talking to the United Nations," he said, criticizing as "a little evil" that children would be propaganda props. "That is an insult to science."

Dr. William Happer, a world-renown physicist from Princeton University who has advised President Trump on climate issues, also denounced warming alarmism and the demonization of C02. In an interview with the New American, Professor Happer said there was nothing to worry about from alleged man-made global warming or human emissions of the gas of life (C02). "C02 will be good for the Earth," Happer said, adding that C02 levels were unusually and extremely low by historic standards.

The New American reached out to the IPCC for comment repeatedly during the recent UN COP24 "climate" summit in Katowice, Poland. However, the organization did not respond to emails. Phone calls, or visits to the IPCC booth at the climate summit seeking comment.

What about unpredictable weather? Do you think that the fact that magnetic North moving 30 miles a year as stated earlier could have something to do with that? How about the damage caused by hurricanes in coastal regions having a dollar cost far in excess of anything prior? That too, is easily explained. More people live near the coast now than ever before and everything costs more because money is worth less thanks to the Banksters that control our very money. What about islands in the South Pacific like Tuvalu being inundated with sea water? Islands in the South Pacific rise and fall all the time. Sometimes appearing for three or four days then sinking into the ocean from whence they came. The Pacific's tectonic plates are the most dynamic in the world. What about Venice, Italy flooding. Venice is sinking, that is an undeniable fact. Did you know that underwater volcanic activity can cause islands to sink? Sciencemag.org has the following article titled, Ship spies Largest Underwater Eruption Ever. The article is dated May 21, 2019. It says that off the coast of Madagascar a new underwater volcano was discovered. The article goes on to say the thing was huge. What really astonished the scientists was the fact that it formed in 6 months. The people of a nearby island called Mayotte new for months something was happening.

There were a lot of earthquakes. The result, the island of Mayotte sunk by 13 centimeters and moved 10 centimeters east in one year.

What about droughts? Droughts have come and gone since time immemorial. Here are some examples. Lake Elsinore is the largest natural lake In Southern California. When it was first discovered in 1810 it was described as little more than a swamp. In the late 1862 it grew much larger, such that the oak trees around it stood in 20 feet of water. Then there was drought from 1862-1865, cattle and horses were dying from lack of water. Then in 1872 the lake was overflowing. In 1950 the lake ran nearly dry. Then in 1960 it was refilled by rain. Let's go back further in time to a different part of the world. You've probably all seen pictures of Petra in the country of Jordan? The ancient city with the pillars carved right into the mountain. The earliest recorded history of Petra was from 312 BC. Petra was a huge trading mecca linking the East, the Middle East, and the West. As you can imagine all those people needed a great deal of water. Petra had an elaborate system of conduits, dams and cisterns to control the water and to protect them from flooding. There was that much water. Why did the inhabitants abandon the city in the 8th century? Because the climate changed. The rains stopped falling in sufficient quantity to support the population. I'm pretty sure no one was driving SUV's back then. In 1829 Western Australia had a drought so severe that that in nearly destroyed all agriculture forcing settlers to traverse long distances for water and pastures for their flocks. In 1630 there was a tree year drought in India that caused the death of more than 2 million people. In 1850 Australia got hit with drought again it was considered one of the worst droughts in Australian history. The 17th century Sahel Droughts were considered some of the most extreme in recorded history. How many times does the bible say; there was famine in the land? The famine was caused by droughts. Most of these droughts that I mentioned happened before the industrial revolution.

Why do multibillion dollar banks keep lending in South Florida right on the ocean? They don't seem too worried about it. What about the Obamas buying a $15 million home on Martha's Vineyard? Martha's Vineyard is an island. The house is reportedly between 3 and 10 feet above sea level, either the Obamas forgot all about climate changes "existential threat" or they simply don't believe it. Hmm.

My neighbor was walking his dog the other day. I asked him what he thought of manmade global warming. He said something quite succinct, simple brilliance I believe. He said, we are not that big." That got me thinking, so I did a little research. According to the U.S. census bureau, in 1950 the U. S. had a population of 150 million. We drove 73% of the world's cars. There were 25 million cars in the U. S. at the time. That was 70 years ago. The rest of the industrialized nations had far fewer cars and third world countries had a miniscule amount not worth mentioning. I then started thinking about the fact that the Earth is 71% ocean.[30] I don't think a lot of cars or factories are in the ocean. I then thought about the vast stretches of dessert in the 29% of the earth we don't inhabit from a carbon fuel burning perspective. The Sahara Desert of Africa, The jungles of equatorial Africa and the vast grasslands in Africa below the jungles. The Gobi desert of Mongolia, the Arabian Desert, vast areas of the Stan countries, (Afghanistan, Kazakhstan, Kyrgyzstan, Pakistan, Tajikistan, Turkmenistan and Uzbekistan) with the exception of small areas of Pakistan these nations, some of them quite large, are living much as they did prior to the industrial revolution. Then we have vast stretches of the South Western United States. How about our Midwest that literally feeds the world. It is so large a college professor of mind once told me you could put the whole of Ukraine's farm area (the biggest in Europe) and have lots of room left over. Then there are huge areas of Australia, you may have heard of the outback? What about Antarctica, the North Pole and Siberia. Alaska is huge, the population of Alaska in 2019; 735,720, not a lot of cars or factories there. Canada is bigger than the United States even including Alaska. It only has a population of 31 million. About one tenth that of the U. S. What about the Great Lakes in Canada and the United States? They are visible from space. They are all huge and are not part of the 71% of the Earth's surface of oceans. Then there's Lake Baikal in Russia. Then of course we have the Amazonian Rainforest. These are all places where mankind is not burning quantities of fossil fuel to be worth mentioning. In secular National Geographic Magazine I read an article from years ago about the Boreal Forrest. The magazine called it the third set of lungs for the planet. The other two being the Amazon and the oceans being the biggest. Which brings us to the carbon cycle.

To begin with CO2 is called the gas of life by scientists. Not the gas of death as the Globalists want you to believe via their bought and paid for fake news

---

30   Oceanic Institute.

and scientists not willing to have their science be peer reviewed. Here is what NASA has to say about carbon. Carbon is the backbone of life on Earth. We are made of carbon, we eat carbon, and our civilizations-our economies, our homes, and our means of transportation- are built on carbon. Most of the earth's carbon is stored in rocks, about 65,500 billion metric tons.[31] The earth is a closed system. There is a finite amount of carbon on/in the planet. Do you think that the carbon in the rocks is going anywhere? Did you know the carbon cycle speeds up and slows down depending on the amount of carbon in the atmosphere? When the atmosphere has more carbon plants grow faster. Plants are of course built on carbon. We eat plants. We eat animals that eat plants. We store carbon in our bodies as do plants and animals. When biological organisms die the carbon is released into the atmosphere to then be used by plants to grow. The ocean is the second largest reservoir of carbon on the planet. Since the ocean is where we get the majority of our oxygen that means that algae and other sea plants are exhaling oxygen as they inhale CO2. The carbon in the atmosphere is used over and over again. Just as rain comes down, then reinters the atmosphere via evaporation or transpiration. That is a simplistic view of the carbon cycle. We are not big enough, even if C02's effect on climate was accurate according to the computer models that are proven time and again to be wrong. With all this common sense and science in mind do you still believe that we're facing an existential threat in 12 years?

The Globalists want a worldwide carbon tax. This gives them more control of industry. This kills jobs. A carbon tax would force million to rely on government handouts of food because there are no jobs. This then gives the government more control. This is worldwide. "A government big enough to give you everything you want is strong enough to take away everything you have." Thomas Jefferson. The Carbon Tax would be sold to us because our survival depends on it. There are too many people exhaling CO2. There are too many people to feed. Nature is out of whack. Population control is a must. Sorry, no children for you, we have too many. We are going to need to sterilize you for the good of the world. Sound crazy? It already happened! You may say that had to be Nazi Germany right? Right, but only after it happened right here in the good ole United States. That's right, the Eugenics movement was in the U. S. first. The early Eugenics movement received extensive funding from The Rockefeller foundation. From 1907

31   NASA, https://earthobservatory.nasa.gov/features/carboCycle.

to 1963, 64,000 people were forcibly sterilized in the United States, this from History.com, Nov,15 2017 . There are tons of sources for what you are about to read. None of this is new. Like many other important subjects it is not taught in public schools. Forced sterilization is a matter of historical fact. Those sterilized were poor Whites Americans, Native Americans and African Americans, among others. It surprised me to learn that W. E. B. DuBois had some beliefs that aligned with eugenics. He believed that in developing the best versions of African Americans in order for his race to succeed. The whole concept gets even more whack. Some men were forcibly sterilized because they were deemed too aggressive. Who makes that decision? How do they make it? He hit the tennis ball too hard, he's got to go? How about CFR member Bernie Sanders saying we should withhold aid to nations that don't practice birth control. First it starts with the poor, then it moves up the social economic scale. You may be thinking forced sterilization was a long time ago. It is a matter of historical fact that in 1975 Indira Ghandi, the then prime minister of India declared a national emergency. She seized dictatorial powers, imprisoned her political rivals, and embarked, with the help of her son Sanjay, on a mass, compulsory sterilization program that registers as one of the most disturbing and vast human violations in the country's modern History.[32] Most sources say that between 6 and 8 million men were forcibly sterilized. By now you should know who provided the money. The Ford and Rockefeller Foundations. Here is what Robert McNamara, (mentioned earlier) former World Bank President had to say about it. "At long last, India is moving to effectively address its population problem." The Rockefellers have long been fans of culling the herd, your permission is not needed. Earlier I wrote that the Rockefeller family controls Mickey. There is a YouTube video from 1968 aimed at our children, staring Donald Duck which talks of the horrors of a large family.[33] When we speak of things like sterilization in the early and late part of the last century we think it couldn't happen now. It couldn't happen to me. Poor people here and in third world nations are the guinea pigs. This bring one of my favorite quotes to mind. "First they came for the socialists, and I did not speak out because I was not a socialist. Then they came for the trade unionists, and I did not speak out because I was not a trade unionist. Then they came for the Jews, and I did not speak out, because

---

32   https://www.google.com/amps/s/www.vox.com/platform/amps/future-perfect-/2019/5/18629801/ emergency-in-india-1975-indian-ghandi-sterilization-ford-foundation.

33   https://m. youtube.com/watch?V=t2DkiceqmzU.

I was not a Jew. Then they came for me, and there was no one left." Martin Niemoller. Nothing Changes, certainly not mankind.

President Trump pulled the United States out of The Paris Agreement on climate. He was lambasted by the press. China signed up. China is the biggest polluter and C02 omitted on this planet. The agreement would kill industry. Estimates are that it would cost the U. S. one trillion dollars the first year. Do you really think China, a country that steals intellectual property and constantly manipulates the value of its currency would adhere to the agreement?

Earlier I stated there is a manmade ecological threat. Anyone remember Fukushima? On March 11th, 2011 a massive tsunami hit the Fukushima Daiichi Nuclear power plant in the Fukushima prefecture of Japan. There are 6 reactors there. Three sustained severe damage. All three cores largely melted in the first three days. To put it plainly three reactors severely damaged rather than one as in Chernobyl. According to the BBC between 112,000 and 125,000 people have died as a result of the Chernobyl melt-down as of 2005. How many people died since 2005 as a result of radiation is anyone's guess. The Chernobyl accident was April 26, 1986. Chernobyl is on land not near the ocean. The area around Chernobyl is still a no go zone. Fukushima sits right on the Pacific. That's a major problem given that Japan has more earthquakes than any other country in the world by an extremely huge margin. Japan sit on the ring of fire. It has 20% of the world's earthquakes with a magnitude of 6 or better. Japan is the size of California. Considering its small size that's a lot of earthquakes. The manufacturer of the nuclear reactors, GE. The cooling units of the three damaged reactors no longer function. This means that tons of water must be pumped into the reactors every single day to keep them cool. That water then becomes contaminated. Up until late 2018, 3 to 4 hundred tons of water was seeping into the Pacific…every day. The amount of water escaping into the Pacific has now been reduced to approximately 150 tons a day. There are two huge problems. One, the radioactive water being used to cool the three damaged reactors must be stored in giant tanks. The tanks are the size of oil tanks you see around oil refineries. The tanks were hastily built and some are beginning to leak. They must build one every three or four days. On top of that, the area around the damaged reactors is finite. By 2022 or so, there will be no more room to store the radioactive water. The Japanese have discussed releasing the water into the ocean. The outcry from their own fishermen was enormous. So far that has not been done. What happens in 2022 when they run out of space around Fukushima? An aerial view of Fukushima will bring home the magnitude of the problem. You can see it on the net. The second more immediate threat is the 3 to 400 tons of water a day already released into the pacific. Remember that went on for nearly 8 years. There are still 150 tons being leaked into the Pacific today and every day. TEPCO (Tokyo Electric power Company) was able to slow it, but it cannot be stopped. Dr. Helen Caldecott is an extremely well respected anti-nuclear activist and writer. She has written some brilliant books on the matter. Her book: Crisis With No End is a must read regarding Fukushima. Listening to her speak on Fukushima is a revelation. She tells us that South Korea will not accept food from Fukushima. She goes on to say that the Japanese are mixing Fukushima food with food grown in other areas of Japan because the Japanese want nothing to do with Fukushima food. The mixed food is then labeled with a deferent prefectures name. As of November, 2019 nothing can be done to stop radioactive water from leaking. Humans can't go into the reactors, they would die in 2 minutes, even while wearing the best suits that can be made to protect them. Robots get fried in about the same amount of time. That's how high the radiation levels are. Helen Caldecott's book tells us much more than that. As you can imagine children and the elderly (the most vulnerable) are already feeling the effects. Thyroid cancers are beginning to go through the roof. No one can stop the radioactive water from entering the Pacific, the largest ocean in the world. The Pacific is vast you say. It's being diluted. here is a quote from Dr. Caldicott. "Solution to pollution by dilution is fallacious." The radioactive material is not going anywhere. Some of the isotopes have half lives of thousands of years. Unfortunately there's more. The Japanese are storing the radioactive soil substances from the "cleanup" in plastic bags, outside! The recent typhoon that hit the island in late 2019 dispersed the bags all over the prefecture. Dozens cannot be found. Is that not nuts? It makes you wonder who's running that circus. You don't hear this in our news, nor do the Japanese hear it in theirs. Here's the dirty secret of the nuclear industry: It takes 5 to 60 years for the radiation you got from a piece of fish in Fukushima to give you cancer. The cancer doesn't come with a Made In Fukushima stamp. So the nuclear industry can point to literally hundreds of other places, food or things you may have gotten your cancer from. So we have a tiny island that has 20% of the world's magnitude 6 earthquakes or better and some genius decided that would be a good place to build nuclear reactors. So... there is our true environmental threat.

I know that manmade climate changed has been pounded into our heads. I know repetition is the mother of learning. I urge you all to consider looking up Global cooling and scroll around. As I said, the body of scientists supporting the evidence is growing all the time. I believe the climate change button is so hot right now to not only attack President Trump and frame him as a Climate change denier, and thus cost him votes. It is also hotter than ever right now because if some type of climate tax legislation is not passed very soon it will have no chance. I believe we are already in a global cooling phase.

Christians and those of the Faith of Judaism believe in climate change. We learned about it in the book of Genesis. Genesis 7:11 and 7:12 tell us the following. In the six hundredth year of Noah's life, in the second month, the seventeenth day of the month, the same day were all the fountains of the great deep broken up, and the windows of heaven were opened. And the rain was upon the earth forty days and forty nights. That was the first great climate change; a worldwide flood. It had never rained before. Genesis 1:1 tells us the following. And God said, let the waters under the heaven be gathered together unto one place, and let the dry land appear, and it was so. And God called the dry land Earth; and the gathering together of the waters called he Seas: and God saw that it was good. The gathering together of the waters in one place. That means if the water was in one place then the land was in one place. Bear with me. We are about to get to our planet as we know it. You've all probably noticed that the world looks like a puzzle. South America and Africa fit together. Many areas of the earth look as though a puzzle was simply spread apart. Modern science tells us that the Earth was once all one super continent called Pangea. Scientists postulate that moving plate tectonics are responsible for the land mass we see before us today. I believe they got it right this time, makes sense to me. What caused it? I believe the flood. Think about it. Massive amounts of water coming down from heaven and up from wells and fountains. Think of the pressure in the earth's crust being released with the water from the wells and fountains. Think of the weight of the water covering the highest mountains. I believe this caused instability in the earth's crust. Due to this instability we have ever moving (plate tectonics) we see today. Here's an analogy. Scuba divers are taught as they descend to blow threw their nose as they pinch it. This equalizes the pressure in their head to the surrounding pressure of the ocean. Every ten feet a diver must equalize the pressure in his head because of the pressure on his head. If a diver doesn't equalize his head to the pressure of the water he is in, his head will literally implode. The earth, after the flood, had no pressure equalizing mechanism. Remember water from above as well as water from below came pouring out from the earth and down from the heavens. Thus the division of the earth into the continents we see today. Genesis 10:22-25 has this to say. The sons of Shem: Elam, Asshur, Arphaxad, Lud and Aram. The sons of Arum: Uz, Hul, Gether and Meshech. Arphaxad was the father of Shelah, and Shelah the father of Eber. Two sons were born to Eber. One was named Peleg, because in his days the earth was divided: his brother was named Jokton. Peleg was a great, great, great grandson of Noah. In Peleg's day the Earth was divided, not people, the earth. Some believe that the continents as we know them today happened during the flood. Some believe that the separation of the continents happened in Peleg's day. I believe the later account, that the earth was literally divided in Peleg's day. Some Theologians believe that the verse, "Because in his days the earth was divided," refers to a spiritual divide. Chronologically this does not make sense. It was under the leadership of Nimrod and his wife Semiramis that the earth was spiritually divided and that the people were divided. Here is what Genesis 11:9 has to say: Therefore its name was called Babel, because from there the Lord scattered them abroad over the whole face of the earth. Nimrod was a great grandson of Noah. The spiritual divide and the scattering of the people happened in Nimrods time, 2 generations before the birth of Peleg. In those days after the flood lifespans were still on the order of a couple hundred years. It is from Nimrod and Semiramis that we get the pagan religions of the Near East, the Far East and the West. For more information on the subject of history just after the flood see Alexander Hislop's extremely well documented book, The Two Babylon's. You will not find it in a book store. You can get it online. For reading of the literal translation regarding the earth being divided in Peleg's day see the following link, I believe it to be a compelling argument.[34] Finally God spoke very clearly which is all we should need. The bible tells us, "For in his day the earth was divided." We are living on a planet that is not as God created it, due to our sin. We are spinning around the sun on a planet that looks much different than it was originally created. God created a planet that had a firmament above, which allowed for near constant temperature. The firmament also protected humans and animals alike from the harmful rays of the sun. God created a perfect world. Climate change has been around approximately 4,500 years, not billions.

---

34   *Https://biblearchaeology.org/research/flood/2887-making-sense-of-the-days-of-peleg.*

What about Dinosaurs and the age of the Earth. In 1966 a movie came out called The Bible: In the Beginning… It had big stars in it: John Huston, Richard Harris, Peter O'Toole, Ava Gardner and George C. Scott, to name some of the bigger stars. In those days bible movies were common and they made money at the box office. I believe that that movie has put some erroneous images in people's heads that were then perpetuated up until now, even in children's biblical comic books. In the movie we see all the animals coming to Noah full grown. Genesis 7:13-16 tells us the animals came to Noah. In the comic books we see giraffes and elephants with their heads sticking up out of the ark. This image leads people to believe that the dinosaurs could not possibly have fit on the ark. This I believe is important. When people doubt one part of the bible it's easy to dismiss the rest as so many made up stories. God instructed Noah to take "all" the animals. What if the animals including dinosaurs came to Noah as newborns? That sure would economize space. Many scientists believe that there were only about 70 different types of dinosaurs with most being the size of American Bison. What happened to the dinosaurs? Then God blessed Noah and his sons, saying to them, be fruitful and increase in number and fill the earth. The fear and dread of you will fall on all the beasts of the earth and all the birds of the air, upon every creature that moves upon the ground. And upon all the fish of the sea: they are given into your hands. Everything that lives and moves will be food for you. Genesis 9:1-3. The animals had the fear of man imprinted upon them. We've all heard how dangerous a cornered animal is. Can you imagine a cornered T-Rex. I believe that the more vicious dinosaurs were killed after the flood and some possibly before. They may have been killed because of the danger they posed to the post flood world. The vegetation eaters may have simply become extinct as a result of predation or lack of sufficient food in a world that was only very recently covered up to the highest mountains in water. Perhaps many of the dinosaurs simply died because they were designed for a pre flood world. A world that had a constant temperature. Remember Adam and Eve were walking around naked after creation. Perhaps the dinosaurs could not survive the new climate phenomena called seasons. If we are to believe that they were reptiles they would have needed a certain amount of warmth from the sun to survive. Perhaps some of the dinosaurs after the flood did not migrate towards the equator soon enough and died because they could not stay warm. In an article from Creation.com, creation 19 (4):42-43, dated September 1997 titled Sensational Dinosaur Blood Report, we learn the following. Actual red blood cells in bones from a Tyrannosaurus Rex? With traces of the blood protein hemoglobin. It sounds preposterous-to those who believe that these dinosaur remains are at least 65 million years old. In the article scientists from Montana State University found red blood cells in a Trex. The article goes on to state that Dr. Margaret Helder alerted readers of Creation Magazine to documented finds of "fresh," fossilized dinosaur bone as far back as 1992. The evidence that hemoglobin has indeed survived in this dinosaur bone (which casts immense doubt upon the "millions of years" ideal is to date, as follows.

The tissue was colored reddish brown, the color of hemoglobin, as was liquid extracted from the dinosaur tissue.

Hemoglobin contains heme units. Chemical signature unique to heme were found in the specimens when certain wave lengths of laser light were applied.

Because it contains iron, heme reacts to magnetic fields differently from other protiens-exracts from the specimen reacted in the same way as modern heme compounds.

To ensure that the samples had not been contaminated with certain bacteria which have heme (but never the protein hemoglobin), extracts from the dinosaur were injected into rats, if there was even a minute amount of hemoglobin present in the T. Rex sample, the rats immune system should build up detectable antibodies against this compound. This is exactly what happed in carefully controlled experiments.

Evidence of hemoglobin, in the still recognizable shapes of red blood cells, in fossilized dinosaur bone is powerful testimony against the whole idea of dinosaurs living millions of years ago. It speaks volumes for the bibles account of a recent creation.

Any secular scientist will tell you that crocodiles have been around for 65 million years. Those same scientists will tell you that T. Rex lived 70 to 65 million years ago. The same scientists will tell you that there was some cataclysmic event that wiped out the dinosaurs. What about the Crocodiles that were around at the same time? Why didn't the cataclysmic event wipe them out? This whole theory of a billion year old earth has more holes in it then my spaghetti strainer. Secular Scientists shoving a billion plus year old earth theory detract from the truth in the bible.

What about carbon 14 dating?

Carbon 14 dating is used to date once living things (organic material) it cannot be used to date rocks. Because of the rapid rate of decay of Carbon 14 it can only be used to date once living material in the thousands of years and not millions. It cannot be used to date rocks. What about ancient rocks proving a billions year old earth? Now we are talking of radioisotope dating. Mount Ngauruhoe is located in the North island of New Zealand and is one of the most country's most active volcanos. Eleven samples were taken from solidified lava and dated. These rocks were known to have formed from eruptions in 1949, 1954 and 1975. The rocks were sent to a respected laboratory (Geochron Laboratories in Cambridge, Massachusetts). The "ages" of the rocks ranged from 0.27 to 3.5 million years old.[35] The laboratory was off by just between hundreds of thousands of years and three and a half million. The old earth pseudo-science is pushed by the globalists to break down the Judeo/Christian beliefs' this country was founded on. This makes it easier to shove man made climate change down our throats and then create industry killing regulations so that the government can control us. Getting rid of God is paramount as well. The state must be God. There is no God in N. Korea, China or any other totalitarian regimes.

Bakersfield, California is 134 miles from the Pacific Ocean. There is a place there called Sharktooth Hill. It's a bit of a tourist attraction where shark teeth are found on a daily basis. Shouts of Meg can be heard when someone pulls up a huge shark tooth. I think there are only two ways to explain Sharktooth Hill. One, there was a global flood, I'm going with number one, or two, the sea levels were much higher. If the sea levels were so much higher than any of the climate models theorize they could be in 2100, why is there life on this planet? One last point to ponder. In Popular Science magazine, in an article by Kiley Watson dated February 25, 2020, we have an article written that appears to agree with a worldwide flood. The article states that 80% of the faunal remains found in the Sahara, specifically the region around Southwestern Libya, were fish. That's a far cry from the merciless desert it is today. The article then goes on to state that about 5,000 years ago it all dried

---

35   *Answesingenesis.org. By Mike Riddle, October 4, 2007.*

up and we have the Sahara as we know it. So we have yet more evidence of massive climate change millennia before SUV's and jet airplanes.

Remember the Globalist media says that sea level rise is an existential threat. The Globalist media knows repetition is the mother of learning/brainwashing and they will drum this into our heads until the dinosaurs come home. Because you hear something on the news or read it in a magazine does not make it true. We must all apply the lost art of critical thinking.

I know that it is extremely difficult to get beyond the constant barrage of manmade climate change. The articles are everywhere in print and on all fake news networks on a daily basis, from morning till night. On top of that we have Hollywood scientists (actors) telling us how we need to live and attacking President Trump whenever they can. So here is a quick synopsis to have handy when the need arises to help out a brainwashed person... like I was.

The sun has high and low energy cycles. Low energy cycles mean mini ice ages as we had circa 1450. People starved.

High energy cycles give us the heating we experienced up until a few years ago.

Many scientists, some from NASA, are saying the sun is going into a cooling cycle.

Scientists warning of the potential crop failures from a cooler sun are saying to scientists that are denying cooling "here is our science show us yours."

Magnetic North is moving 30 miles a year. There is no debate here, scientists agree on the movement. They agree it effects global weather patterns.

Scientists agree that magnetic storms effect weather patterns.

Underwater volcanos are heating the oceans and glaciers. New underwater volcanos are being discovered all the time, some by accident.

70 percent of all volcanos are underwater.

Some Glaciers are now growing.

Many scientists claim we just had the two coolest years in over a decade.

Many scientist say there is a poor correlation between CO2 and warming.

We have an IPCC scientist saying that scientists are being bribed for ulterior motives.

All Gores models about catastrophic warming and rising sea levels did not happen. The movie came out 14 years ago. They are all wrong.

The Obamas just bought a multi-million dollar home on an island three feet above sea level.

Chapter 4

NAFTA

"What congress will have before it is not a conventional trade agreement but the architecture of a new international system…a first step toward a new world order." Henry Kissinger, July 18, 1993 in Writing in the LA Times, speaking of NAFTA.

Kissinger is not only a CFR member he is also a Bilderberger.

NAFTA was established Jan.1, 1994. CFR member Joe Biden in the democratic debates is fond of saying I know how to create bipartisan cooperation to get things done. It has not escaped my attention that when the Globalist puppeteer politicians want something bad for the United States, party lines are never a problem. Such was the case with NAFTA. Republican George H. W. Bush constructed it and Democrat Bill Clinton got it passed. NAFTA is a train wreck! It is also a huge step toward what many call the American Union, the melding of Canada, Mexico and the United States. Just like the EU, where there is one currency, no trade barriers, no borders except on a map, unelected officials and no God in the new constitution that would replace our own. The U. S. constitution is the best document written by citizens, for citizens, to protect citizens from the government, ever created. It is a huge problem in the way of A New World Order. Our founding fathers where quite aware that government was something to keep a watchful, vigilant eye upon. Thus they purposely divided the government into three branches. The Judicial, the Legislative and the Executive, checks and balances. President Trump has appointed over 150 Federal judges. His choices are labeled as conservatives, not the constitutionalists they are. The term conservative is a nice Globalist twist on realty. NAFTA was sold to the congress and the American people as a Godsend to increase trade and make the citizens of the three nations involved (The United States, Canada and Mexico) more wealthy. It would create jobs. It turned out to be a job killer. Nothing was done about it until President Trump came along. I remember him saying, "The people that created NAFTA were bad deal makers." I don't think he knew how bad the swamp was at that time. When you look at all the deals that were made with foreign countries for the last 70 years the vast majority were not good for America. This was not an accident. Gary Allen in his book, The Rockefeller File put it something like this, if our politicians were trying to do the right thing, shouldn't the odds of chance dictate that they get it right at least half the time? So where do we start with this train wreck called NAFTA? Let's start with drugs, the illegal kind.

Thomas Homan the former Immigration and Custom Enforcement Chief tells us that the Northern Mexican border is completely controlled by drug cartels. Drugs are pouring across our border with Mexico in Mexican trucks. Here's an article in Vice, hardly a right wing source. The article is by Joe Tone dated January 4, 2019. It' states that between 1994 and 2001 the number of trucks crossing into the U. S. from Mexico nearly doubled to roughly 4.3 million per year. U.S. border control agents could only inspect ten percent of these trucks, leaving a big opening for drug traffickers. A decade after NAFTA , 90 percent of Columbian cocaine was smuggled through the southwest border. Mexico, which had always been the Walmart of marijuana and heroin, quickly became the Fed Ex of the cocaine business. The article goes on to say that NAFTAs impact on the global drug trade and on the massive wealth and power accumulated by Mexican cartels and kingpins in indisputable. Here is an excerpt from Ryan Grim's book, "This is your Country on Drugs" The Secret History of Getting High in America.

During the first year of his administration, President Bill Clinton made free trade a top priority, pushing for the passage of NAFTA. It wasn't an easy task. Having helped the democrats take the white house for the first time in 12 years, organized labor was in no mood to see manufacturing jobs shipped to Mexico. The debate was difficult enough without having to talk about the sprawling Mexican drug trade and its attendant corruption (I'm adding here, on both sides of the border), and how the agreement would end up benefitting the cartels. So he ordered his people not to talk about it. Clinton knew from the beginning that drugs would pour across the border and told his people not to talk about it. This does not sound to me like a president who has his people's welfare in mind. The article goes on to say, "we were prohibited from discussing the effects of NAFTA as it related to narcotics trafficking, yes." Phil Jordan, who had been one of drug enforcements leading authorities on Mexican drug organizations, told ABC News reporter Brian Ross four years after the deal had gone through. "For the godfathers of the drug trade in Columbia and Mexico, this was a deal made in narco heaven. The first year after NAFTA went into effect cocaine from Mexico made a 25% jump from the year before. The number of meth related emergency room visits in the United States doubled in between 1991 and 1994. In San Diego, America's meth capital, meth seizures climbed from 1,409 pounds in 1991 to 13,366 pounds in 1994. For those of you not familiar with San Diego it is a border town just north of Tijuana Mexico. The southwestern border towns were and are not the only cities in America to be devastated by the free flow of drugs into the U. S. do to NAFTA. Because of NAFTA Mexican and Canadian truckers no longer had to offload the cargo to be picked up by American truckers within twenty miles of the U.S. northern or southern border. They could now drive their cargo all over the U. S. without an American driver's license! Yep, crazy but true.

I have to say this, lest you the reader get the wrong impression. I grew up in an area of southern California where Mexicans were the majority. I am not prejudiced against Mexicans. The first time I had Mexican food at a friend's house at 8 or 9 years of age I thought I died and went to culinary heaven. I have multiple family members that are Mexican. I have several friends that are Canadian. I'm talking about bad trade agreements and there effects on our country whether you be Mexican, Canadian, Italian, Black, Asian, Pacific Islander or whomever else I've missed. I didn't speak about drugs from Canada because cocaine grows in South America and comes up through Mexico, thanks to George H. W. Bush and Bill Clinton who got it passed and George W. Bush and Obama who did nothing about it. They did however incarcerate black and brown people in record numbers. I am prejudiced against Globalists, unashamedly so.

How about the effect on our domestic trucking industry? The following is from Public Citizen. NAFTA's service sector chapter included a requirement that all three countries highways be fully accessible to vehicles of trucking companies based in any NAFTA nation by 2000, an item pushed by large U. S. trucking firms seeking deregulation and lower wages. NAFTA also recommended but did not require, that Mexican, Canadian and U. S. truck safety standard be harmonized. (I.e. made uniform). That provision had no deadline, nor did it require Canadian and Mexican standards be brought up rather than U. S. standards brought down. The U.S. Department of Transportation's Inspector General conducted studies that repeatedly revealed severe safety and environmental problems with Mexico's truck fleet and drivers licensing. For instance, Mexico's commercial driver's licenses permitted 18 year old drivers, required no drug testing nor did the government have a system for tracking violations, insurance or hours of service. Let's think about this for a moment. I don't know a whole lot of 18 year olds that have any business behind the wheel of a big rig and a fully loaded trailer. In my mind that's a huge safety issue. There is a reason auto insurance premiums don't begin to decline until a driver turns 25. The insurance actuaries clearly show that young drivers get in disproportionately more accidents. The owners of huge American trucking firms liked NAFTA because with an influx of cheap drivers they could now pay there people much less. The truckers were some of the first people to feel the wage killing effects of NAFTA. Even if some of the large trucking firms wanted to protect their drivers how would they compete with Mexica/Canadian trucking firms that paid lower wages and did not have to spend money bringing their trucks up to U.S. environmental standards. NAFTA made the cost of doing business higher for U.S. trucking firms, how many jobs do you think that cost U.S. truckers?

What about the environmental impact? As crazy as this sounds Canadian and Mexican trucks do not have to meet our emission standards. The car you and every other American drives must meet emission standards. It is the same with American trucks. This is a huge cost that Canadian and Mexican trucks do not have to absorb, again, making them more competitive. Even since 1995 when NAFTA trucks were restricted to a 20 mile zone at the borders, there has been a surge in crime, drug trafficking and air pollution from lines of trucks that can run several miles long during peak periods as trucks wait to enter the U. S. Increased truck traffic has been the leading cause of deteriorating air quality at 13 border cities and has been linked to high levels of respiratory disease in children in border communities, according to Government Accountability Office, a government oversite agency. Now we have these trucks running all over our nation. All of these facts were known a decade and more ago. Challenges were made in court in three different administrations. They failed to improve the train wreck. Open borders are a major step towards Globalism.

What about all those jobs NAFTA was going to create? Here's an article from Robert E. Scott dated November 2003. This article appeared in the Economic Policy Institutes website at epi.org. It is titled, The High Price of Free trade. Here is an excerpt. Since NAFTA was signed in 1993, the rise in the U. S. trade deficit with Canada and Mexico through 2002 has caused the displacement of production that supported 879,280 U. S. jobs. Most of these jobs were high wage positions in manufacturing industries. The loss of these jobs is just the most visible tip of NAFTA's impact on the U. S. economy. In fact, NAFTA has also contributed to rising income inequality, suppressed real wages for production workers, weakened workers collective bargaining powers and ability to unionize, and reduced fringe benefits.

Another huge step toward the American Union and globalism is NAFTA's ability to have U. S. laws challenged and defeated in court for the greater good, not the greater good of our country but of other countries and their corporations. According to Public Citizen NAFTA was negotiated behind closed doors with hundreds of corporate advisers, NAFTA was radically different than past trade deals that focused on traditional trade matters, like cutting border taxes,. Instead, most of NAFTA's new provisions grant new powers and privileges to multinational corporations. These new powers make it easier for corporations to outsource jobs and attack the environmental and health laws on which we all rely. NAFTA's investor protections create incentives for corporations to relocate production and jobs elsewhere. NAFTA also guts the Buy American policy that requires the government to buy American made goods when spending our tax dollars. This outsources our tax dollars rather than investing them to create jobs here. Is it any wonder that one of President Trump's campaign promises was to renegotiate NAFTA? That is exactly what he did. Nancy Pelosi let it wallow on her desk for a year. It seems obvious that President Trump has the American people's best interest at heart and Nancy Pelosi does not. NAFTA also rolled back food safety protections. Before NAFTA we only imported meat and poultry that satisfied U. S. safety standards. NAFTA requires the U. S. to accept meat and poultry imports that satisfy Canadian and Mexican standards, which was declared equivalent to U. S. standards even though there are significant differences that threaten safety. At the heart of NAFTA were investment outsourcing protections and new rights for multinational corporations to sue the U. S. government in front of a tribunal of three corporate lawyers. These lawyers can order U. S. tax payers to pay the corporations unlimited sums of money, including for the loss of expected profits. Train wreck. The corporations only need to convince the lawyers that a law protecting public health or the environment violates their special NAFTA rights. The corporate lawyer's decisions are not subject to appeals. You just can't make this up. Any third grader knowing what you've just read would say "no way". This corporate power grab is formally called Investor State Dispute Settlement (ISDS). Taxpayers have paid hundreds of millions of dollars under NAFTA to multinational corporations over toxic bans, environmental and public health policies, and more, with tens of billions pending in ongoing cases. Another chapter gave big pharmaceutical firms new protections against competition so they can raise medicine prices. This is one of the reasons health became a mess. We know that NAFTA was bad for not just American jobs but public safety and the environment. From a job and wage standpoint it was bad for Mexican farmers, very bad. More than 2 million Mexicans engaged in farming and related work lost their livelihoods as NAFTA flooded Mexico with subsidized corn and other agricultural products. We are talking about small family farmers. Some historians call such farmers the backbone of a strong economy. Tens of thousands of small retail and manufacturing firms were bankrupted as NAFTA opened the door to Walmart and other mega retailers. Real average annual wages in Mexico are now lower than they were before NAFTA, and those making the least were hurt the most (always),with the minimum wage declining 14%. NAFTA supporter's warnings about the chaos that would engulf Mexico, and a new wave of immigration from Mexico, if NAFTA was not implemented have indeed come to pass, but ironically because of the devastation of many Mexican livelihoods occurring because NAFTA was implemented.

Here are a few quotes in 1993 from Bill Clinton followed by reality.

"I believe that NAFTA will create 200,000 new jobs in the first two years of its effect...I believe that NAFTA will create 1,000,000 in the first five years of its impact". Here is the reality. According to the Economic Policy Institute the net job loss in America was 1,000,000 in the first ten years of NAFTA alone. Contrary to popular belief the job losses were not just in the Rust Belt but nationwide. El Paso Texas had the highest job losses recorded. The two states hit the hardest were California and North Carolina. According to The Bureau of Labor Statistics 4,500,000 U.S. manufacturing jobs have been lost to NAFTA since it took effect. These jobs were not lost to automation.

"With NAFTA, U. S. exports to Mexico will continue to outstrip Mexican Imports to the United States, leading to a U. S. trade surplus with Mexico". Gary Hufbauer and Jeffery Schott, NAFTA an Assessment, 1993. This was the study that was universally cited by the Clinton administration and congressional and corporate NAFTA supporters. Here is the reality. According to the U. S. International Trade Commission in 1993 the U. S. had a $3 billion U.S. goods trade surplus with Mexico and a $31 billion deficit with Canada the year before NAFTA took effect. By 2017 the U. S. had a combined trade deficit of $191 billion with Canada and Mexico. That is a 576 percent increase.

"NAFTA will create more jobs, increased exports and higher wages with the agreement than without" Don Newquist, chair of the International Trade Commission. The reality; NAFTA put downward pressure on wages and exacerbated domestic inequality. The broadest impact of NAFTA has been on the quality of jobs and thus the lack of wage growth for the 66 percent of U. S. workers without college degrees.[36] About two out of every five manufacturing workers who lost jobs and were rehired in 2017 experienced a wage reduction, according to the Bureau of Labor Statistics. About one out of every four took a pay cut of more than 20%. Companies' threats to outsource to Mexico under NAFTA have weakened workers bargaining power and contributed to the widespread stagnation of wages. After NAFTA, for example, U. S. companies' became more likely to threaten to outsource jobs to Mexico as a means of defeating union organizing drives, or otherwise restrain or cut wages or benefits for U. S. workers in union contract negotiations.

The standard of living in Mexico will become closer to that in the U. S. as labor conditions and wages in Mexico will improve. "NAFTA insures the Mexico enforces it's laws in area that include worker health and safety, child labor and the minimum wage… it means that there will be an even more rapid closing of the gap between our two wage rates" Bill Clinton 1993. Now what compassionate human being could argue with that salesmanship? It's for the kids will get people every time. The reality: Mexico's real wages have decreased, and per capita GDP has barely risen, and labor conditions for children and adults did not improve. Overall, in real terms average annual

---

36   http://www.census.gov/data/tables/2017/demo/education-attainment/cps-detailed-tables.html.

Mexican wages are down 2%, and the minimum wage is down 14% from pre NAFTA levels.[37]

Environmental conditions in Mexico will improve. "In a few moments, I will sign side agreements to NAFTA that will make it harder than it is today for business to relocate solely because of very low wages or lax environmental rules. This side agreement will make a difference. The environmental agreement will, for the first time ever, apply trade sanctions against any of the countries that fails to enforce its own environmental laws" Bill Clinton 1993. The reality: Environmental conditions deteriorated. NAFTA's environmental obligations proved entirely ineffective. No enforcement orders or sanctions have resulted from the 91 submissions seeking enforcement of environmental violations that were filed before NAFTA'S Commission on Environmental Cooperation.[38]

So what happened in Mexico, Canada and the U. S. was the shrinking of the middle class and huge money being made by multinational corporations at the cost of food safety, worker safety, wage reduction and environmental protections. The U. S. had 8 years under Clinton a Democrat, and 8 years under George W. Bush a Republican, and 8 years under Obama a Democrat to fix NAFTA, none of them did a thing. I'll say it again, we have an illusion of choice between Democratic and Republican presidential hopefuls, and they have all been Globalists. It is interesting that President Trump is attacked regarding the environment, and yet in his first two years in office, with no help from Democratic leaders that are either Globalists or are simply trying to not lose their job to a Republican challenger riding on President Trumps' coattails, that no one in the legislative branch of the government has done anything about it, NAFTA. The media certainly didn't report on this train wreck. But I digress, the mainstream media is controlled by the Globalists by their own admission.

It's no wonder that the American public is held in such low esteem by the puppeteers that control our politicians. For a century they have been lying to us and we keep signing up for more. They know with their control of the media we can be made to believe anything. I'm sure they thought it hilarious

37 *Organization for Economic Cooperation and Development.*

38 *Commission for Environmental Cooperation, Article 14: submissions on enforcement matters," updated June 25, 2018, accessed Dec 11, 2018. Available at:http://www,cec.org/sites/default/files/ documents/sem-process=status-en.pdf.*

that after 4 years of George H. W. Bush's lies we elected his son to lie to us some more. If they hadn't fallen off their chairs with that one, eight years of Bill Clinton lies and then we nearly elected Hillary, that must have done it.

Getting rid of NAFTA was one of the campaign promises President Trump made. A campaign promise made and kept…like many others.

Chapter 5

The U. N.

Ostensibly the U. N. is an altruistic world body to end war. It past and current actions tell a very different story. According to Megan Roberts the Associate Director of the International and Global Governance program at the CFR, the United States pays 22% of the U. N.'s budget. Given the fact that there are 193 nations who belong to the U. N. it seems to me that we might be paying more than our fair share to a Globalist organization who has failed time and time again, since its inception in 1945, to create world peace. The good news, President Trump has slashed our funding of the U. N. That 22% by the way does not include voluntary contributions. Voluntary contributions prior to President Trump often were more than the 22% the United States was mandated to pay. So what did we pay in 2017 before President Trump slashed our payments? The United States paid a mandatory 10 Billion in 2017, more than the next three largest contributors, Germany, UK and Japan combined.[39] We will soon see that the U. N. has not and cannot be held accountable for rape and murder. Do you think it possible that a good part of your tax dollars are disappearing with zero accountability? Anyone remember the U. N. Oil for Food program? Congress's Government Accountability Office, has estimated that Saddam Hussein siphoned at least 10 billion from the program by illicitly trading in oil and collecting from companies that had United Nations approval to do business with Iraq. Multiple investigations then underway in Washington and Iraq and at the United Nations all center on one straightforward question: How did Mr. Hussein amass so much money while under international sanctions? An examination of the program, the largest in the United Nations

---

39   Quartz.com, A Simple Guide to how the U. N. is funded, by Amanda Shendruk, September, 2019. https://qz.com/1712054/who-funds-the-united-nations/.

history suggests an equally straightforward answer: The United Nations let him do it.[40]

The U. N. headquarters is in Lower Manhattan. As stated earlier the land was bought and donated by the only son of John D. Rockefeller. John D. Rockefeller Jr. (January 29, 1874-May 11, 1960). Jr. donated the land and the American taxpayer was signed up to pay for the building. We were not asked. The U.N. is not about peace, it's about the fleecing of every countries national sovereignty. Part of the money for the food and hygiene supplies given to the various migrant caravans on their way to the U. S. was supplied by the UN. There were NGO's involved as well, one of which was funded by CFR billionaire George Soros. The UN does not want national borders. It should be noted that 42 members of the United States delegation to form the U. N. were, had been, or would later become members of the CFR.[41]

Here is an article from The Dallas Morning News dated Jan 18th, 2019, by Claudia Rosett. The entire article can be found at https://www.dallasnews.com/opinion/comentary/2019/01/18/the-united-nations-is-trying-to-grab-control-of-worldwide-immigration-policies/. The article starts out, A new United Nations Plan would undermine America's sovereignty and control over its own borders. And, yes, if the UN has its way America will pay for it. While President Trump seeks funding for a border wall, the UN is seeking control of migration worldwide, with a campaign to undermine America's sovereignty over its own boarders, (Once again we have President Trump doing battle with the Globalists.) As with many of the UN's turf grabs this campaign to co-opt national migration policy has been years in the making. Incremental in its origins, and swaddled in UN jargon and procedure, it has largely escaped US headlines. But it has now reached the stage of becoming dangerous. The spearhead of the UN campaign is an international agreement with the high minded name of the Global Compact for Safe, Orderly and Regular Migration. That's not remotely what this document boils down to. While proclaiming a utopian "unity of purpose" among the 193 highly diverse member states, this Global Compact would have the UN's largely unaccountable, self-aggrandizing and often opaque bureaucracy, operating in service of its despot-infested collective of governments, set the terms for all.

---

40 *The New York Times by Susan Sachs and Judith Miller August 13, 2004.*
41 *Robert W. Lee, The United Nations Conspiracy, Appendixc, p.242.*

The lengthy text reads like a template for setting up the world's politically correct welfare state, with a colossal menu of entitlements and central planning for migrants: never mind the costs to the pockets, rights and freedom of existing citizens. This "compact" does not restrict itself to refugees. It anoints the UN as arbiter of how to handle cross border human mobility worldwide, meaning migrants, permanent or temporary, whatever their reasons for wanting to move. In this scheme of the universe, the UN proposes to become the overreaching authority "addressing migration in all its dimensions." Coming from a UN that has yet to solve its own problems with peacekeeper rape of minors, that's ambitious.

In a section on eliminating "all forms of discrimination," this compact aims to "shape perceptions of migration," not least by smothering free speech and promoting gags and penalties for news coverage or debate the UN., in its collective majesty, deems unfriendly to migrants. This conference was adopted without a vote at an international conference in December, 2019 in Morocco, in which the U. S. declined to take part. The resulting draft was endorsed on December 19th by the UN General Assembly in New York, over U. S. protests.

It is telling that of the 193 member states. The 152 countries voting in favor of the compact include such brazen human-right abusers as Russia, China, Cuba, Venezuela, Myanmar and Iran. The five countries voting no were the U. S., Israel, Poland, Hungary and the Czech Republic. The remaining 36 member states either officially abstained or did nothing.

At the U.N., such big vote tallies in favor of U. N. turf grabs are business as usual. In practice, the Global Compact would entail virtually no cost for rogue, despotic or failing member states, which routinely vote for resolutions they themselves ignore. The main costs would fall on law abiding, free countries that provide the most desirable destinations for migrants, and notably on the biggest single contributor to the U. N., the United States. The U. S. mission to the U. N. denounced the compact, accurately, as amounting to a bid "to advance global governance at the expense of the sovereign rights of states to manage their immigration systems in accordance with their national laws, policies and interests. Authors note: Thank God for Trump and Nikki Haley. I'm quite sure Hillary would have signed us up in a heartbeat. A U. S. envoy warned that that this compact could translate into a "long-term of building customary international law or so-called soft law in the area of migration," and expressed particular concern that the term "compact" is an amorphous word in international law, "but implies legal obligation."

The U. N. rejoinder has been that General assembly resolutions are nonbinding; participation by member states is voluntary.

Which brings us to the real pressure tactics with which the U. N. is attempting to end run around the United States. In concert with a vision outlined in 2017 by Secretary-General Antonio Guterres, the compact itself calls for the U. N. to set up a sprawling "network on migration," to embed, coordinate and promote the compact's methods and goals throughout the U. N. system and around the globe. The U. N. terms of reference for this compact include a preliminary list of 38 U. N. entities already slated to promote this agenda.

The compact further stipulates that the secretariat and coordinator of this migration network will be a U. N. agency called the International Organization for Migration. The IOM operates with a staff of more than 9,000, in some 150 countries, with a budget of more than 1.4 billion per year, the biggest slice of that contributed by the U. S. The kicker is that it was three years ago that the IOM joined the U. N. For some 65 years before that, it was chiefly led, bankrolled and shaped by the U. S., and served as one of Americas most reliable partners in dealing with immigration. Based in Geneva, the IOM was founded in 1951 as an intergovernmental agency-outside the U. N. system. The migration organization was not a policy shop. Its mission was primarily to help with logistics in resettling displaced people in Europe by WW2. That led to it helping migrant populations hit with both manmade and natural disaster, from the Soviet invasion of Eastern Europe, to the boat people, to victims of the Christmas tsunami in 2004, and so forth. The IOM cooperated with the U. N., but in keeping with longstanding U. S. preferences, it did not join the U. N. The arrangement worked pretty well. That all changed under President Barack Obama. During Obama's final year in office, in 2016, with a nod from his administration, the IOM joined the U. N., which promptly declared plans to create a global plan for migration. For 2017, as a parting gift of the Obama administration, America's $544 million contribution included $1.68 million earmarked for conferences and consultations supporting the creation of the Global Compact. Authors note: (Americans never heard anything about this in the Globalist controlled media.) In late 2017, the Trump administration reversed that policy, announcing the U. S. would no longer support U. N. activities leading to the Global Compact. Ambassador Nikki Haley released a statement that: "America is proud of our immigrant heritage and our longstanding moral leadership in providing support to migrant and refugee populations across the globe," but the U. N.'s global migration project is simply not compatible with U. S. sovereignty."

It is interesting to me that President Trump, in the last year or so has been using the phrase "I'm not a Globalist," more and more. I certainly believe him. The border wall provides us ample proof, again, I believe that the extent to which the Globalists have nearly achieved their goals was surprising even to a United States President. A non-Globalist president at any rate.

In August, 2018 President Trump withdrew 200 million in aid to the Palestinian Authority. The reason had to do with what is called "Pay to Slay." The PA is paying terrorists that carry out attacks against Israel. The Pay to Slay money is paid to families of imprisoned terrorists and even those killed why committing acts of terror. The families of suicide bombers get paid as well. Why would any country in their right mind pay for terror? Fortunately President Trump disentangled us from that bit of evil. Canada, Australia and the Netherlands among other nations followed suit. This left the PA without sufficient funds to pay their terrorists. So what did the U. N. do when the PA approached them and said they needed 355 million for "humanitarian needs," the peace loving U. N. helped them raise the money. The U. N. wants anarchy. Fear is a powerful tool of control for the Globalists. The question becomes, how much freedom are you willing to give up for security? This question is being asked everywhere around the globe. The anarchy and fear is being created by the very people that are offering "security and peace."

The following can be found in The Guardian, by Ed Pilkington Oct. 1, 2019. The article states that UN peacekeeping forces were directly responsible for a Cholera outbreak that killed 10,000 Haitians and infected hundreds of thousands more. The victims are petitioning the U. S. Supreme Court to hold the U. N. accountable. The heart of the question is this: should a world body (the UN) be answerable in domestic courts for the harm it causes people it is there to serve. The UN has admitted that cholera was introduced to Haiti by peacekeepers returning from Nepal. Basic health measures could have been taken to prevent the transfer of the disease at the cost to the UN of only $2,000. Raw sewage was allowed to be dumped from UN camps directly into rivers used for cooking and drinking water. This all happened in 2010. No compensation has been paid by the UN. The UN further states that it has total immunity from such claims relating to the harmful impact caused by its staff carrying out routine business. So the UN is saying that its people can basically defecate on people of any nation with impunity.

The UN peacekeeper were not quite done abusing the Haitians. In an article by Skye Wheeler dated 1-11-20 appearing in The Hill, we learn that the UN peacekeepers were also raping Haitian women. The Associated Press and other media outlets have published credible reports of sexual abuse and exploitation by the UN peacekeeping force in Haiti for years. The UN left in 2017. Credible reports of rape have also come from Somalia, Central African Republic, and the Democratic Republic of Congo. The article goes on to say that prosecutions have been rare.

Speaking of the Congo. In June of 1960 the Congo was granted independence from Belgium. Two power blocs emerged to rule the country. One was led by an anticommunist named Moise Tshombe . The other was led by a drug using Communist named Patrice Lumumba. Lumumba after taking power allowed his soldiers to go on a murderous rampage including rape. This first bit of his legacy was against the European residents. The European settler's bank accounts were frozen and basically stolen by Lumumba. The Belgian government sent troops in to protect what were at that time citizens of Belgium. At this time Tshombe was fighting against the animals let by Lumumba as well. The U. N. intervened. Would you believe that the United States, siding with Russia ordered the Belgium Army out of the country? The forces led by Lumumba then went on another murderous rampage this time even raping and killing nuns. The thousands of U. N. forces that had recently poured into the country did nothing. These were the same peace keeping forces we see all the time with the blue berets all the time. After witnessing all this and with insufficient forces to stop the bloodshed and outer chaos. Tshombe led a province called Katanga and tried to secede. At first he was successful with the help of the returned Belgium army. Things in the Katanga Province were near normal…peace had been restored. It was then that the U. N. showed its true colors. United Nations forces attacked the peaceful Katanga Provence! The Katanga provincial army fought back against the U. N. "peacekeeping forces." They fought well. Some estimates say that 90 percent of the buildings destroyed by the U. N. were civilian.

During the fighting the white settlers fought on the side of their Katanga neighbors. Together they drove the U. N. back. The U. N. then agreed to a cease fire. The U. N. tried to paint the people of Katanga as savages in the media. The problem was too many U. N. peacekeepers were caught on film committing atrocities. Almost one year later the U.N. peacekeepers were back for more death and destruction. This time supplied with American dollars and war material. The people of the Katanga province could not hold out. A few years later Congo was a pawn of the Globalists. Its resources and that of many other African nations were now available for pillage by the very powers controlling the U. N. all the time. Sadly the United States was first among the pillagers.

What's the point of U. N. Peacekeepers if they allow rape and murder, participate in rape and sexual exploitation and certainly don't keep the peace? Source after source tell us that the U. N. has been accused in multiple countries throughout the world of rape and sexual exploitation numbering in the thousands. We learned earlier that they have no oversite and no accountability. A worldwide army, well-funded, well-armed, with no accountability. In what world is this good for humanity? A few more examples if you are not yet convinced.

Rwanda 1994: Hundreds of desperate Tutsis sought refuge on the first day of the genocide at a school where 90 U. N. troops were under the command of Captain Luc Lemaire. Here they were safe from the Hutus and their machetes. The U. N. flag flew over the school. The Belgian peacekeepers were armed with a machine gun, planted at the entrance. These soldiers were the world's army. The Tutsis could not imagine that they would stand by why they were slaughtered. The 39 year old captain feared otherwise. The U. N. in New York had ignored warnings that the genocide was being planned and the Security Council was pulling out peacekeepers in response to the mass killing.

Within days, the U. N. command decided there was more important work for Lemaire and his men than protecting the Tutsis. The peacekeepers were ordered to abandon the school in order to escort foreigners to the airport and out of Rwanda. As the soldiers left, Tutsis begged to be shot rather than left to the militia's machetes. Within hours, the 2,000 people at the school were murdered by gun, grenade and blade.

Lemaire's contingent kept a sporadic video diary of the wretched event. At one point a shaky captures a sandbagged machine gun post and a pickup truck of Hutu militiamen sweeping by. The video then focuses on the soldiers' log. It Reads: "New York didn't agree to change the rules of engagement." The peacekeepers were not allowed to save the Tutsis. The camera's microphone picks up an anonymous voice: "There are killings and New Yok doesn't give a damn."

The betrayal of the Tutsis in Rwanda was a low point for U. N. peacekeeping but not an isolated one. A year later, Dutch peacekeepers failed to stop the massacre of 8,000 Muslims in Srebrenica, a supposedly U. N. "safe area," the most notorious killing by Serbs in Bosnia.

Not long before, there had been the debacle in Somalia where a U. S. led U. N. humanitarian mission turned into a bloody conflict against a powerful warlord. By then Angola was already back at war after its U. N. peacekeeping mission was already back at war after its U. N. peacekeeping mission collapsed amid accusations it contributed to the breakdown of peace.

Other disasters-the Democratic Republic of Congo (again), Sierra Leone-were still on the horizon even as the U. N. peacekeeping budget doubled and doubled again with growing numbers of missions. There were good reasons to question the point of U. N. peacekeeping in the 90's and to wonder if it was not costing as many lives as it was protecting by offering an illusion of security. The murdered Tutsis might have stood a better chance had they fled to Uganda. Two decades later, those responsible for U. N. peacekeeping- U. N. officials, countries on the security council assigning missions, militaries contributing the forces in blue helmets/berets-say the lessons of the 1990's have been learned.[42] The above sentence mentions the countries on the Security Council and the fact that they are learning their lessons. There are five that are permanent. They are: The United States, United Kingdom, France, Russia and China. The other ten rotate every two years. How is the U. N. going to "learn Lessons" when three of the five permanent members (the U. S., the U. K. and France), are ideologically opposed to the other two, Russia and China? It is also interesting that these five permanent members of the peacekeeping Security Council are all part of the top ten biggest arms

---

42   *The Guardian September 17th, 2015, by Chris McGreal. https://www.google.com/amp/s/amp.the
      guardian.com/world/2015/sep17/un-united-nations-peacekeepers-rwanda-bosnia.*

dealers/exporters in the world. The U. S at number one followed in order by Russia number two, France number 3, China number 7 and the United Kingdom at number 8. Germany is number 4 in the export of weapons. Their weapons are being made by the same families/corporations that made war material for the first two World Wars.

Here's another example of U. N. failure, this time from the BBC. This is from January, 2017. The article is titled: The U.N.'s peacekeeping nightmare in Africa. One of the key issues facing Antonio Guterres. the U. N.'s newly installed secretary-general, will be to address critical failures in African peacekeeping operations. With this in mind, he will surely be asking himself whether the vast origination he is now leading needs to chart a different course. The bulk of U. N. money goes to Africa. The U. N. spends 8 billion on peacekeeping efforts...or lack thereof.

A new report by the Geneva –based research group Small Arms Survey has accused the U. N.'s mission in South Sudan (Unmiss) of lacking neutrality by giving arms to rebels in the town of Bentiu in 2013. It blames Unmiss for underreporting arms confiscated from fleeing soldiers and handing over the weapons to soldiers of the Sudan People's Liberation Movement-in Opposition (SPLM-IO) on more than one occasion. The report also claims that shortly after this transfer of arms, the rebels went on to carry out a massacre of civilians. The operations of the U. N. in South Sudan came into sharp focus after embarrassing revelations that its troops failed to protect civilians following clashes between government sources and former rebels in July 2016. A damning internal investigation found that its peacekeeping mission in the capital, Juba, had failed to achieve one of its core mandates, namely "to protect civilians under threat of physical violence, with specific protection of women and children." It described the troop's response as chaotic and ineffective. At that time the U. N. had 13,000 peacekeepers deployed on South Sudan. Eyewitnesses said women and girls were raped near U. N. compounds with no action from the peacekeepers. Not far away, foreign aid worker suffered similar sexual violence at their residence. Their case gained much international condemnation, but it is dwarfed by the scale of the atrocities South Sudanese civilians have long suffered.

In February, gunmen killed 30 internally displaced people and wounded more than 120 others within one of the U. N.'s designated Protection of Civilian compounds in the north-western South Sudanese town of Malakal.

The irony of the facility failing to live up to its name was not lost on the missions critics. The U. N. later accepted responsibility for its failure to prevent the bloodbath.

In the Central African Republic (CAR), the U. N. mission (Minusca) has also been accused of inaction when more than 75 people including civilians' were killed in the north during an outbreak of violence in September 2016. Jean-Serge Bokassa, the interior minister of CAR, accused the peacekeepers of colluding with armed militias. "What is the role of the Pakistani contingent in Kaga-Bandoro?" he asked. "Their collusion with armed groups has gone on too long." A week later 4 people died in the capital Bangui during anti-U. N. protests.

Since we are in the midst of COVID-19 let's see what The World Health Organization (WHO) has done on this particular crisis. Believe me I could cite many abject failures by the WHO but I'm trying to keep this book at 200 pages. The WHO is a specialized arm of the U. N. The WHO has been around since 1948 with 150 offices worldwide. In an article titled: World Health Organization under the microscope: what went wrong with the coronavirus, by Hollie McKay of Fox News, published March 28 we learn some interesting yet not surprising information. As Coronavirus started sweeping from its origin in a Wuhan Wet Market in China late last year, the information coming from the Who was one of dismissal, in line with the Chinese Communist Parties muzzling. The article goes on to say that the WHO was trying to be politically correct. Dr. Attila Hertelendy, a Florida based expert in biomedicine told fox News that the WHO lost credibility when they stated in late January that the global risk was moderate. He goes on to say: "For an international body that people and governments and the business community look to for advice, they are simply too slow, burdened by bureaucracy and political correctness. They have a great staff working for them, and many of my colleagues are advisors, they just need to listen to them and take action swiftly." Dr. Stanley Weiss, a professor and Epidemiology at Rutgers New Jersey Medical School, Concurred that the lack of early action has been frustrating for the medical community." Dr. Weiss is being nice. I'm going to say it plainly, The WHO"S politically correct Bleep has cost lives. The article goes on to state that The WHO waited much too long to declare a Global Health Emergency. A designation that would have alerted public health officials in neighboring countries to prepare. "Similarly the WHO initially refuse to declare a global pandemic, bizarrely claiming that they no longer used this designation, but then they ultimately did so," noted Dr. Dena Grayson, a Florida based expert in infectious diseases. "This also likely caused substantial delays in preparedness by other nations in advance of this deadly virus." It get worse for the WHO.

Brett Schaefer, a Senior Researcher in International Affairs, the Heritage Foundation, said China has "a well-established record of suppressing information that it considers harmful," a notion not new to the WHO. Thus, it is hardly surprising that it failed to be transparent and truthful in reporting details on COVID-19 to the WHO and the international community. In fact this is not the first time this has happened," he said. "In 2003, China concealed and denied and infectious disease outbreak- later called SARS- for months. Given this history, the willingness of the WHO to take China's statements at face value is shocking. The WHO leadership is too susceptible to political pressure in its decision in declaring a public health emergency of international concern, and this needs to be addressed." In 2017 the United States gave the WHO 400 million in voluntary contributions, This is on top of the 10 billion of mandatory contributions the CFR men signed you and I up for. The U. S. is the largest financier of the WHO. The U. S. gives the WHO more money than the U. N. itself.[43]

Taiwan said it alerted the WHO back in December, 2019 about the risk of human to human transmission, the WHO ignored them.

The article goes on to state that the role of the WHO's leader, Ethiopian national Tedros Adhanom Ghebreyesus was tapped for the top job in 2017. I'm wondering why someone who is not even a Dr. is head of the WHO? Some are questioning whether he buttered up to governments like China in return for massive donations to the organization. (You the reader know where I'm thinking some of that money went, based on U. N. corruption already referenced in this book.) Ghebreyesus routinely lauds Chinese President Xi Jinping for his handling of the pathogen, while not acknowledging the early cover-up and the fact that several doctors were muzzled for daring to speak out about a strange new virus percolating in Wuhan. On April,2 2020 the Japanese Deputy Prime Minister, Taro Aso said the WHO should be renamed the China Health Organization. "Early on if the WHO had not

---

43   Https://apple.news/A90xwMVT3RbWlrOSiiCMzuA.

insisted to the world that China had no pneumonia epidemic, then everyone would have taken precautions."

I could go on and on. We have heads of states saying "get the U.N. out." We have people protesting and dying to get the U. N. out. The United States pays the lion's share of the money for U.N. "peacekeeping." It is a horrible investment for many reasons, chief among the many reasons is that we are financing murder and rape. We should stop ALL funding to the U. N. If we want to help a nation, we, The United States, should determine who gets the money and how much.

Here's an article from Adam Shaw of Fox news appearing September 2019. The verbiage President Trump uses is proof that he definitely knows what the U. N. is about and what its ultimate goal really is. The article is titled: Hungary joins Trumps attack on "open borders" agenda at U. N., says "national interest comes first." United Nations-A day after president Trump ripped into the "evil" agenda of "open borders activists" this week and warned that the future belongs to "Patriots," Hungary's top diplomat is offering his support as he prepares to take the stage and accuse U. N. organizations of attacking human rights in their quest to promote migration as a fundamental right. " I believe that the world must understand that national interest comes first and those countries that are ready to act accordingly must not be attacked an must not be unfairly treated, considered and judged," Hungarian Foreign Peter Szijjarto told Fox New on the sidelines of the U. N General Assembly. Szijjarto said when he takes the stage, he will speak about how "dangerous" new waves of migration coming to Europe are in terms of both law and security. "We understand there is a debate within the United Nations and within the debate the real fundamental human rights are ignored and issues which are not matters of fundamental human rights are being falsely portrayed as if they were part of fundamental human rights, meaning that a right to a safe life in your home is a fundamental human right and this is totally ignored and denied by the U. N. organizations and they try to sell migration as if it were a matter of fundamental human rights-which it is not," he said.

The message is similar to that of President Trump, who touted a nationalistic message when he said that "wise leaders always put the good of their own people and their country first." Authors note: These next sentences are quite telling. "The future does not belong to Globalists, the future belongs to patriots." He said. "The future belongs to sovereign and independent nations who protect their citizens, respect their neighbors and honor the differences that make each country special and unique." A little later he had this to say, "Today, I have a massage for those open border activists who cloak themselves in the rhetoric of social justice: Your policies are not just, your policies are cruel and evil," he said, accusing them of promoting human smuggling and the "erasure of national borders."

Szijjarto then had this to say: "We have made it very clear that regardless of any kind of pressure or where it comes from, we keep our borders under 100% control and that's why there are continuous attacks on us, so these activists, NGOs mostly with George Soros in the background, they continuously hit and attack Hungary.

CFR member George Soros has both Hungarian and United States citizenship.

Hungary has committed to making illegal immigration almost nonexistent in the country. Britain, Israel and Brazil are all adopting similar nationalist views. I find it interesting that no one is calling the Brazilians racist.

I'm sure by now you have figured out that I am a Christian. That means I'm a sinner just like the millions upon millions of you that are reading this book. I know some of you may have the following bible verses in mind.

You are to have the same law for the foreigner and the native born. I am the Lord your God, Leviticus 24:22. NIV

When you have finished setting aside a tenth of all your produce in the third year, the year of the tithe, you shall give it to the Levite, the foreigner, the fatherless and the widow, so that they may eat in your towns and be satisfied. Deuteronomy 26:12. NIV

Do not mistreat or oppress the foreigner, for you were foreigners in Egypt. Exodus 22:21

There are many more verses concerning foreigners but I think what we have above will shed some light on this affair from both a Christian and a U.S. Citizen standpoint. The first verse above, Leviticus 24:22 is quite clear, we are to treat the foreigner and the native born equally. That does not mean that foreigners by whatever name you want to call them should get free stuff as the Socialist Democrats are proposing. If citizens in a land have to pay for medical care under the law then foreigners should also have to pay. So the socialists are wrong from a biblical standpoint when pandering for votes by promising free medical care, this is achieved by catch, release, and vote. I think it is crazy that some form of I. D. is not required to vote. The second verse, Deuteronomy 26:12 say every third year we should give a tenth to the Levites the widows, the fatherless and foreigners. I assure you the United States does that every year, regarding the foreigner at least, via foreign aid and the cost of immigration to this nation. More on that in the next chapter. The Exodus verse speaks of not mistreating a foreigner. Properly vetting foreigners and being sure that the kids actually belong to the adults they came here with is not oppression, despite what the nut jobs want you to think. Lastly, the Lord gave us all freedom of choice. Requiring citizens to tithe is not biblical. Every family has the God given freedom of choice to tithe as they see fit.

From a United States Constitutional standpoint they are wrong as well. The framers put it this way in the first amendment to the constitution, it reads like this: Congress shall make no law respecting an establishment of religion, or prohibiting the free exercise thereof.

The United Nations, like any government agency gets bigger and bigger. This means every nation must pay more and more to keep the bloated bureaucracy thriving, and growing yet more. The United States, again, is the main supplier of good ole fashioned money. The mandate of the U. N. was sold to the world shortly after World War Two with the following grandiose, altruistic babble. "The last hope of mankind… the only means to protect the world from the horrors of war." Let's have a very brief look at how the U. N. has grown like an all-consuming virus on civilization. Here are some of the organizations under the U. N. umbrella that you and I pay for, what many of these organizations have to do with peace I have no idea.

FAO Food and Agriculture Organization of the United Nations

UNWTO World Tourism Organization

ICAO International Civil Aviation Organization

UPU Universal Postal Union

IFAD International Fund for Agricultural Development

WHO World Health Organization

ILO International Labor Organization

WIPO World Intellectual Property Organization

IMF International Monetary Fund

WMO World Meteorological Organization

IMO International Maritime Organization

IBRD International Bank for Reconstruction and Development

ITU International Telecommunication Organization

IDA International Development Association

UNESCO United Nations Educational, Scientific and Cultural Organization

IFC International Finance Corporation

UNIDO United Nations Industrial Development Organization

The above organizations are under the Principle Organ called the Economic and Social Council. There are five other U.N. Principle Organs, they are: General Assembly, Security Council, Secretariat. International Court of Justice and the Trustee Council. These five other Principle Organs have another 52 bodies or commissions like the ones listed above. With all these organizations under the U. N. banner that means all these people working for these various organizations must be paid by our tax dollars, our tax dollars given with zero accountability. Once again, If they can't be held accountable for rape and murder, how, with all these various bodies doing who knows what, would anyone be able to track where the money is going?

If the U. N. peacekeeper were actually physically preventing war, why is it that only 3,000 have died since 1945?[44] This is out of a force that since at

---

44   Peacekeeping .UN.org.

least 2015, numbers over 100,000 year after year. So I ask again, how are they preventing war? It is certainly not U. N. condemnation, Israel is the size of New Jersey, and there have been more condemnations and resolutions against Israel than any other country on Earth. When comparing the relatively small death toll (if such a thing can be said) in all Israeli armed conflicts since its inception in 1948, the fact that it has drawn so much animus from the U. N. seems to support a U. N. political agenda. Especially compared to the carnage in Africa. Since the inception of the U. N. there have been over 300 wars and 3,000 other military conflicts, with nearly as many people killed as in WW2.[45]

The U.N. is an abysmal failure in its "stated goal" of world peace. Meanwhile tax payers all over the world are paying hard earned money to an organization that is corrupt and has no accountability. When nations are given money to help them in any fashion the U. N. gets to "wet its beak" through corruption and the paying of its bureaucracy. If the U. S. or any nation is going to give money to a deserving nation, the nation giving the money should determine who gets it. It should then give it directly to that nation. That would leave more money for the receiving nation having eliminated a needless, corrupt and failed bureaucracy whose goal is Globalism.

---

45   *the Trumpet, from the booklet, He Was Right https://www.thetrumpet.com/literature/ read/7094=he-was-right/447.*

Chapter 6

President Trumps Alleged Xenophobia and the Wall

$274,126,340,096

The above number is the cost of Illegal immigration in 2019. This information comes from One America News Network. Their sources were provided by the center for Immigration Studies, the Department of Homeland Security, the Federation for Immigration Reform, the Institute for Defense Analysis, Yale and MIT. President Trump asked for 5 billion to build the wall. I'm not a mathematician but I'm pretty sure that spending 5 billion and saving the American Taxpayer 269 billion is good math. The wall is being built despite what you don't hear on the fake news, another campaign promise kept. President Trump has managed to build well over 200 miles as of June, 2020, despite constant roadblocks from a congress that can't do simple math as stated above. Here is a nine minute video showing the wall being built, it is pretty interesting,[46] President Trump is being accused of Xenophobia because of his stance on illegal immigration. If they sneak into this country they are not undocumented migrants, they are illegal aliens. "All Americans, not only in the states most heavily affected, but in everyplace in this nation, citizens are rightly disturbed by the large numbers of illegal aliens entering our country. The jobs they hold might otherwise be held by citizens or legal immigrants. The public services they use impose a burden on our tax payers. That's why our administration has moved aggressively to secure our borders more by hiring a record number of border patrol guards, by deporting twice as many criminal aliens as ever before, and by cracking down on illegal hiring, by barring welfare benefits to illegal aliens." The person I am quoting used the term criminal aliens. Is that racist? It is when

---

46   *https://www.youtube.com/embed/RJ6FX1_yXJU.*

President Trump says it. The quote above is from Bill Clinton, a man never accused by the press and the Globalist talking heads of racism. Clinton then goes on to say, "we are a nation of immigrants but we are a nation of laws." Obama more than 8 years later said much the same thing. So close in fact that it appears to be the same writer. Neither of these fake news media darlings were accused of racism or xenophobia. Here is the two and a half minute video so you can see for yourself.[47]

So what is President Trump's motivation for saving the American Taxpayer 269 billion a year, beside 269 billion? Since we are in the midst of a worsening Coronavirus let's see what the CDC had to say about our borders. I say had, because I'm going to site the CDC from 2011 to take Coronavirus out of the equation. Leaving it in would just be too easy. It would also not shed light on the fact that the porous southern border was a danger before Covid-19 and that were the wall not to be built, a porous southern border would be a danger long after Covid-19. Let's keep in mind that Mexico, as of March 2020, has closed its southern border. They must be Xenophobic as well.

The following is from an article on the CDC website, it is titled Borders, Budgets, and the Rising Risk of Disease, July 6, 2011 by Ali S. Khan. The article starts out by saying that the perfect storm may be brewing. 27 million people pass through El Paso Texas alone, every year. Obama cut Federal Funding by 50% in the early Waning Infectious Disease Program. Texas is second in the nation for number of tuberculosis cases, the majority of which are found near the border and many of the cases involve tuberculosis strains that are drug resistant. The reason the strain is drug resistant is because infected Mexicans are not getting proper treatment on their side of the border. I am not blaming them. I am simply pointing out a problem with the Mexican Government not taking care of its people, I have no ill will towards Hispanics of any kind, I have Hispanics in my immediate family. Now that you know about the tuberculosis problem, is it any wonder we need to control our borders? You have to ask yourself why Obama would cut funding when the CDC and other health organizations have been saying for decades that porous borders are a huge risk for the next pandemic. So since the Obama budget cut the staff has to "do more with less" to safeguard not only the communities living along the border, but the nation itself. Someone crossing our border with an infectious disease can be anywhere

---

47   *https://m.youtube.com/watch?v=RXwnlsNFXIY.*

in our nation in 36 hours, much less if he or she has an airplane ticket. I'll say it again, the Globalists want open borders. The presidents you have been voting for with the exception of President Trump have been doing their bidding. They do not care about you or your children's health. They do not care what shade of white, brown, black, yellow or red you are.

The Obama administrations unrelenting focus on open borders has exposed Americans to deadly diseases and has politicized the public health agencies that are charged with task of protecting Americans- the Centers for Disease Control (CDC), the National Institute of Health (NIH), the Department of Health and Human Services (HHS), and the Department of Homeland Security. Rather than putting the health of Americans first, these agencies, which once took their roles to protect the public seriously, now go to great lengths to ensure that foreign nationals from countries with serious diseases are allowed to freely enter the United States. And they only act to protect the public when forced to do so by public pressure.[48] The above article was written in 2014. I find the last paragraph quite telling as well as prescient.

At one time the role of the federal government was to protect American citizens by controlling the nation's borders and protecting its citizens from public health hazards. Up until the time of president Trump it seems that the federal government is more interested in pursuing an open borders policy regardless of the dangers it poses to its citizens. Is it any wonder that confidence in the federal government and national leaders is at an all-time low? We now know what the Obama/Biden Administration did not do to protect Americans. Here are some Biden lies (as of March, 2020) the very nature of which are hypocritical in terms of the above articles.

The following comes to us from Bizpacreview.com. Former Vice President Joe Biden has repeatedly pushed misinformation about the COVID-19 coronavirus in political attacks on President Trump and his administration. Biden, has sought to politically capitalize on the coronavirus pandemic. On at least five different occasions, Biden and his campaign have spread misinformation about the President and his administration's response to the virus. Biden (and the fake news media) falsely said President Trump slashed the CDC budget. "We increased the funding of the CDC." "We increased the HIH budget…he wiped all that out…he cut funding for the entire effort,"

---

48   https://cis.org/MOrtensen/Open-Borders-Threat-Puplic-Health.

Biden said at the Feb. 26, 2020 debate. Former 2020 democratic candidate Mike Bloomberg made a similarly false accusation during the debate. They are both wrong to say the agencies have seen their money cut," noted the AP in a fact check of the comments.

Biden falsely said Trump rejected WHO tests. "The World health Organization offered the testing kits that they have available and to give it to us now. We refused them. We did not want to buy them, Biden stated during a March 15th Democratic Debate. But that wasn't true. "The WHO never offered to sell test kits to the United States," PolitiFact said in its fact check of Biden's comments.

Biden's campaign video falsely said President Trump called the virus a "hoax" at his February 28th campaign rally in South Carolina. On March 30th, Biden tweeted a video that misleadingly spliced together President Trump saying "Coronavirus" flowed by "this is their new hoax." In reality President Trump said that Democrats political reaction to the virus was a 'Hoax.' The video makes it seem like President Trump is calling the disease a hoax, which he hasn't done. The words are Trumps, but the editing is Biden's," PolitiFact noted, rating claim as "false."

Biden's campaign falsely accused President Trump of silencing a CDC official.

Biden's campaign produced a video falsely accusing Trump of silencing a CDC official who warned the public about coronavirus. But that wasn't true at all, as the Washington Post noted in a fact check. Wow, things are really bad if even the Globalist Washington Post is claiming false. In the video, Biden campaign advisor Ron Klain claimed the Trump administration silenced CDC official Nancy Messonnier. Klain claimed that Messonnier had been sidelined from briefing reporters after delivering a widely discussed warning about the virus's impact on American lives. "but Klain's framing of the Messonnier situation is simply wrong," the Posts fact check noted, adding that Messonnier continued briefing reports for weeks after the statement in question. The Post awarded four out of five Pinocchio's to the Biden campaign's false claim.

Biden falsely said he hasn't criticized the President's Coronavirus response.

Biden falsely said on "The View" that he hadn't criticized Trump on coronavirus. "I've not been criticizing the president, but I've been pointing out where there's disagreement on how to proceed," Biden asserted. "The coronavirus is not his fault, but the lack of speed and alacrity with which to respond to it has to move much faster." Biden was sharply critical of Trump before his appearance on "The View," and he's continued launching criticism after the interview. Donald Trump' is wholly unfit to lead this nation-and that has become even clearer in the last few weeks," Biden wrote in a tweet before the interview.

Biden's campaign didn't return a request for comment on these facts. Biden is lying so he can become president. He is lying to you.

So we have the Democratic front runner lying and the fake news reporting what he says as fact. The people that are getting their news solely from ABC, CBS, NBC, MSNBC and CNN are being lied to on a constant basis. Is it any wonder that some of them feel about President Trump the way they do? There will be a list at the end of this book for trustworthy news sources.

What about drugs coming over the Sothern Border. We've all heard of the thousands upon thousands of deaths due to fentanyl. Fentanyl is 80 to 100 times stronger than morphine. The drugs first came to our nation via China. President Trump put a stop to that via his tough stance on China. The slack was picked up by Mexican Cartels. Not only is it entering our Nation from Mexico it is now being produced there. The Drug Enforcement Agency (DEA) is alerting the public of dangerous counterfeit pills killing Americans. Mexican drug cartels are manufacturing mass quantities of counterfeit prescription pills containing fentanyl, a dangerous synthetic opioid that is lethal in minute doses, for distribution throughout North America.[49] We know from our chapter on NAFTA that with its advent the rates of Mexican trucks crossing our border exploded. With that explosion came an explosion of drugs of all types. They came right through our ports of entry, the trucks having false bottoms could then go wherever they wanted in our country. The border agents could not inspect them all. This went on for over two decades, and then came President Trump.

---

49   dea.gov/press-releases/2019/11/04dea-issues-warning-over-counterfeiprescription-pills-mexico-0.

As of march, 2020 there is yet another caravan on its way to The United States. I have no doubt in my mind that some of the people in these caravans are fleeing violence in their country of origin. My heart goes out to them. I mentioned earlier that the U. N. and various NGO's were financing these caravans. A little research surprised me by revealing another source. In an article from Real Clear Politics titled, Illegal Immigrant Caravans and Criminal Catholics, Michelle Malkin, a catholic, has the following to say. The article starts out by saying the new caravan is anything but organic. The new caravan number between 2,500 and 4,000, so far. Two weeks ago slickly designed Flyers disseminated on social media beckoned them to sign up for the latest journey and meet at a bus stop in San Pedro Sula, Honduras. That village is caravan ground zero, where Honduras's destabilizing Libre Party and its former top legislator-turned agitator Bartolo Fuentes, have brazenly spearheaded past caravan organizing campaigns since President Trump took office. When they arrived at the Mexico –Guatemalan border young men in the mob threw rocks at police-while sympathetic international "journalists" selectively captured tired women and crying children on the trek with state of the art cameras and livestreams. Make no mistake, these are not desperate people suddenly seeking refuge from violence and harm. They are low wage workers, pew fillers and future ethnic-bloc voters being exploited by Big Business, the Vatican and the Democratic Party. Pueblo Sin Fronteras may be the most recognizable name behind the caravans, but global Catholic elites play a central role in the coordination of this transnational human smuggling racket. Pope Francis donated $500,000 to a fund to assist illegal immigrants. This money subsidizes "27 projects in 16 dioceses and Mexican religious congregations" for "housing, food and basic necessities," As well as 'migrant" assistance programs "run by seven dioceses and three religious congregations, according to the Catholic News Service. The article goes on to say the following: As I have reported in my investigations in Open Boarders Inc., "The Catholic Underground Railroad" of migrant safe house that extend across Central America, through Mexico. And up into the U. S. as a well-oiled machine. The United Nations' International Organization for Migration in Mexico has guaranteed supplies of medicine, hygiene products, construction materials, as well as therapy services and legal training.

So the Catholic Church that has turned a blind eye to the sexual abuse of children for decades, has now determined that the U. S. shall have open borders. If you are Catholic and this offends you I urge you to do your own homework regarding the blind eye statement. I could tell you about the Vatican and Nazi's during and after WW2 but that is not what this book is about. To go further I am not trying to denigrate the Catholic Church, I am merely pointing out facts.

I know that you hear again and again that violence in Guatemala, Honduras and El Salvador is the main cause of these caravans. That bit of "news" is refuted by the migrants themselves. A Guatemalan poll of more than 3,200 households said the following: 91% of migrants surveyed had moved to the U. S. for economic reasons, 0.3% blamed violence, 0.2% cited extortion and 0.2% attributed their decision to gangs.

The risks to immigrants trying to get to the U. S. are not just rape and kidnapping. The risks are a matter of life and death. In August 2019, U. S. Border Patrol agents saved the lives of 28 illegal immigrants as they attempted to cross the Rio Grande River into America. These kind of heroic acts-U. S. law enforcement putting their own lives at risk to save others- are the sort of stories that don't make the fake news. Instead are border patrol agents are portrayed as the enemy. Corporate media profits much more from division and anger than they do from united Americans. These illegal aliens were the victims of human smugglers and included 14 children ranging from 8 months to 17 years of age. After they were left stranded in high current waters, U. S. Border Patrol agents acted swiftly, pulling the Honduran nationals into their vessel and out of harm's way. These individual found themselves in a life threatening situation, which is unfortunate and far too common as smugglers continue to show no empathy for people they attempt to cross illegally into the U. S., Del Rio Sector Chief Patrol Agent Raul Ortiz said. Just about any source will tell you that half of U. S. Border Patrol Agents are Hispanic.

Migrant women are being raped by the very people they pay to get them into the U. S. In an article from the New York Times (of all publications) dated March 3, 2019, by Manny Fernandez, he describes women being locked in rooms by smugglers and being passed around by the smugglers. The article goes on to say that the vast majority of these tragedies go unreported. The article states that this happens to young girls as well. One in three women are raped on their way to the U. S.[50] Now we've got to ask ourselves, why

---

50   *Doctors Without Borders.*

would illegal immigrants brave these kinds of risks? The answer: the U. S. immigration policy put in place by administrations prior to President Trump's. You've all heard the term, "catch and release." If you were caught illegally crossing the U. S. border you were given a notice to appear, usually you were to appear 60 days later. Upwards of 90% of illegals never show up. Instead they disappear into American society. You and I and legal tax paying immigrants that waited their turn get to America get to pay for them. I know that sounds harsh. I know we are all immigrants. My grandparents on my father's side came over on the boat. They went through Ellis Island, legally. There was no welfare or free stuff for them. They were not wanted because they were from Italy and at the time Italians were all crooks and Mafioso. More fake news in that the mafia is Sicilian not Italian. Here's what my Grandparents did before they came here, they learned to speak English. Here is what they did when they got here, they did not speak Italian in front of their children so that their children would be Americans. Incidentally, I think my grandparents were wrong. They should have taught their kids Italian, while they were learning English and with an emphasis on English first. Have you ever thought about the tremendous cost to the tax payer for interpreters in say a courthouse, the DMV and so on? If you have the energy to make a 3,000 mile trek to the U. S. shouldn't you learn the language?

The President of the United States has a primary duty above all others. That duty is to keep Americans safe from outside threats. Do you know that the Border Patrol tells us that individuals from 51 different countries have been found in caravans? The notion that Islamic terrorists might infiltrate by way of the U. S. southern border is not a hypothetical. It has already happened. A captured Islamic State fighter recently related how, in an effort to terrorize America on its own soil, the Islamic terror group is committed to exploiting the porous U. S.- Mexican border, including through the aid of ISIS sympathizers living in the U. S. Whatever one thinks of President Trump's border policy and his claims that it is vulnerable to terrorist, ISIS apparently also thought so.[51] In 2017, for instance, Abdulahi Sharif, originally from Somalia, launched what police in Edmonton, Canada labled a terrorist attack. Sharif stabbed a police officer and then intentionally, it seemed rammed his vehicle into four pedestrians. Sharif had an ISIS flag in his vehicle; he entered the United States and then Canada by illegally crossing the U. S. Mexican

---

51   *Anne Speckhard and Adrian Shajkovc, of the nonpartisan International Center for the Study of Violent Extremism (ICSVE).*

border.[52] From the only public realm reporting, 15 suspected terrorists have been apprehended at the U. S.- Mexican border, in route since 2001. The 15 terrorism associated migrants who traveled to the U. S. southern border likely represent a significant under-count since most information reflecting such border-crossers resides in classified or protected government archives and intelligent Databases. Affiliations included al-Shabaab, al-Ittihad al-Is-lamiya, Hezbollah, the Pakistani Taliban, ISIS, Harkat-ul-Jihad-al-Islami Bangladesh, and the Tamil Tigers.[53] Other Islamic terrorists were eyeing the U. S.- Mexico border long before ISIS came on the scene. Here is just one example. In 2001, federal officials in the FBI and DEA disrupted a plot to commit a "significant terrorist plot in the United States," tied to Iran with roots in Mexico. Months earlier a Jihad cell in Mexico was found to have a weapons cache of 100 m16 assault rifles, 2,500 hand grenades, 100 Ar-15 rifles, C-4 explosives and antitank munitions. The weapons it turned out had been smuggled by Muslims from Iraq.[54] If you still at this point in this book trust the Fake news media, ask yourself why I am telling you this and not them. With all this in mind how do you feel about open borders now? How do you feel about presidential candidates and politicians that attack President Trump on his border policies? The Democratic presiden-tial candidates that attack him on this issue don't care about you or your family's safety. They care about getting elected by using the Globalist Media in a desperate attempt to make President Trump look bad. The democratic congressmen and Senators doing the same, they are simply trying to stay in power by making anything a republican does look bad. All the while there is the fake news.

What about Illegals committing crimes when they sneak into our country? Here is a story that was not reported in the fake news media...at all. This is only the most recent tragedy. A 92 year old legal immigrant from the Dominican Republic was sexually assaulted and killed in February, 2020. This poor women did everything right as far as how she came here and was killed by an illegal. This happened in New York City, a sanctuary city. Her granddaughter spoke at the National Border Patrol Council. Daria Ortiz, the granddaughter of Maria Fuertes cried as she spoke. She said that

---

52 *Middle Eastern Terrorism Coming to the U. S>. Through Its Mexican Border, by Raymond Ibrahim. The Gatestone Institute.*

53 *: Center for Immigration Studies,* November, 2018.

54 *The Gatestone article same author.*

this whole thing could have been avoided had it not been for "sanctuary" jurisdiction, which forbid local law enforcement from cooperating with federal immigration authorities when they issue a detainer---a request that Immigration and Customs Enforcement (ICE) be alerted of any illegal immigrants release from custody so they can be transferred into ICE custody and go through deportation procedures. ICE had a detainer for Khan (the perpetrator) in November 2019, when he had been arrested on assault and weapons charges. But critically that detainer was ignored and Kahn was released onto the streets.[55] Bill DeBlasio is the Democratic Mayor of New York. He has presidential aspirations. He may be aware of the Globalist agenda of open borders. If you had to lay responsibility for this tragedy at the feet of someone, who would you choose? The fake news could not comment on this because it goes against the Globalist narrative in two ways. It shows the real danger of sanctuary cities, and the perpetrator was from Ghana and the victim was from the Dominican Republic. Here's an article from the Heritage Foundation by Hans A. von Sokovsky. He has some startling statistics about crime and illegals. Non- citizens account for 24% of all federal drug arrests, 25% of all federal property arrests, and 28% of all federal fraud arrests. Non-citizens make up only 7% of the population of the U. S. In 2018, 25% of all federal drug arrest took place in five judicial districts along the U. S.-Mexico border.

Can anyone forget Kate Steinle, a 32 year old women walking on the Promenade in sanctuary city San Francisco with her father. She was shot in the back by an illegal immigrant. She did not survive. The shooter, Juan Francisco Lopez-Sanchez had 7 felony convictions. He had been deported 5 times. He was in custody a few months before the shooting. Instead of ICE being notified he was set free to commit murder. Here are just a few of the many stories in newspapers not controlled by the Globalists. The Hill: Mother of son killed by illegal immigrant; We're begging for laws to be enforced. Washington Times : Bill Chemirmir, illegal immigrant charged with killing at least 12. How does this happen? This is madness. I could go on and on. Why should I have to? One murder is too many.

At the beginning of this article I stated that Illegal immigration cost this nation $274,126,340,096 last year. President Trump asked for 5 billion for a wall to protect you and your family. He has been battling with congress

---

55   Fox News, Reported February, 14, 2020.

ever since. Without the help of democrats in congress he has as of now built over 100 miles in key places along the southern border. He chose these places with expert advice from the Border Patrol. He has managed to secure another three billion to really get this wall going. He has done this to protect Americans citizens. President Trump campaigned on this promise. Another President Trump promise made and kept.

Here are just two ideas of what we could do with the 269 billion we are not spending on illegal immigrants. We could build beautiful structures for our homeless Americans, many of whom are veterans, many have mental problems. Many are women. As an ancillary benefit think of how that would stimulate the economy. We would have a ton of money left over. We could then take a vote and see if the American people would like to donate it to the caravan countries. The money would be spent under the watchful eye of The United States, not the corrupt U. N.

Chapter 7

President Trump and
the Racism Smear

"We need to start holding you democrats accountable because they've been taking black peoples votes, and they only talk to black people every four years. All of these politicians only talk to black people every four years because they want their vote. Oh, actually, the republicans don't, the democrats do. But when they get elected, they do nothing in the four years in-between." Charles Barkley.

The republicans want the black vote. They just thought they could not get it. I believe that has changed, because Charles is right about the democrats doing nothing for black people. I think a lot of black people are fed up with the Democratic Party. A bit later we will see what President Trump has done for black people. There have been black leaders for 60 years saying just what Charles said.

Malcolm X had two great quotes that I've gotta put in this book. "If you're not careful the newspapers will have you hating the people being oppressed, and loving the people who are doing the oppressing." I've spoken to a lot of black people about president Trump. By and large the feedback of black people regarding President Trump is overwhelmingly negative. I sincerely wish I was aware of the quote above and below when I had these conversations, it may have opened the door for better conversations.

"You put them first and they put you last. Cause you're a chump. A political chump!.. Any time you throw weight behind a political party that controls two thirds of the government, and that party can't keep the promise that it made to you during election time, and you are dumb enough to walk around continuing to identify yourself with that party-you're not only a chump but you're a traitor to your race." Malcom X.

Everything President Trump does or says has a negative spin put on it by the Globalist controlled media. They know keeping people divided is paramount to their success in enslaving us all. The latest is when he called COVID-19 the Wuhan Virus. No one screams/screamed racism when someone says the Spanish Flu or German measles. It is common practice to call a Flu strain from the name of the place it originated. It gets better. The very sources that smeared President Trump used the same term… before President Trump did. The hypocrisy is never ending. Here is a clip of CNN reporters using the term Wuhan Virus dozens of times, along with ABC and CBS and MSNBC.[56] The clip also shows several interviews of reporters from these very stations doing interviews and calling President Trump Xenophobic. Chris Cuomo is featured prominently, it's a 2 minute or so montage. President Trump caught hell from the media sources above, not to mention Newspapers previously mentioned by saying that Baltimore was rat infested. I'm not sure how that relates to racism but it sure worked for the fake news. Here is what Rep. Elijah Cummings of Baltimore, an African American said during a congressional hearing in 1999. "This morning I left my community of Baltimore, a drug infested area where people were walking around like zombies."[57] Fox carried the video as well. Since Baltimore has a large black population, he was calling black people zombies. Now, which statement is more racist? It's unfortunate that so many politicians don't realize that tattoos are temporary and email, and congressional records, are forever. Ben Carson the African American United States Secretary of Housing and Urban Development, said the same thing regarding rats.[58] Since the name Ben Carson came up, a quick word on what President Trump is trying to do regarding the fact that black homeownership is far behind both white and Hispanic home ownership. What did President Trump do, he went out and found a smart guy to see what could be done, a really smart guy, literally a brain surgeon. His name is Ben Carson.

---

56   https://www.realclearpolitics.com/video/2020/03/12/media_called_coronavirus_wuhan_or_chinese_coronavirus_doxens_of_times.html.

57   Dailywire.comhttps://www.dailywire.com/news/watch-video-emerges-elijah-cummings-calling-ryan-saavedra.

58   https://www.npr.org/2019/07/30746630946/ben-carson-backs-trump-claims-baltimore-homes-were-infested-with-rats-roaches.

There are a large number of black celebrities that are backing President Trump for reelection. To name a few: Kanye West, huge recording artist Bryson Gray, Larry Elder, Candice Owens, and the really fun, smart gals Diamond and Silk. Then there's Stacy Dash, Dennis Rodman, Mike Tyson and Terrell Owens.

Then there's Leo Terrell. Mr. Terrell is a well-known civil rights activist and a lifelong democrat. He is so incensed by the violence being allowed in democratic run cities that he has stated numerous times that the Democratic Party has changed and he will be voting for President Trump.

There is a lot of fear out there among black and Hispanic people when it comes to publically supporting President Trump. It's sad. I remember in 2016 a Hispanic friend of mine said, "Hey Paul, don't tell anyone but I'm voting for Trump." That friend is now 82 and is five foot six. This same friend was one of the few Hispanics on the pro golf tour 50 years ago when golf was lily white. Do you think he dealt with some prejudice? He certainly doesn't think President Trump is racist. Which brings us to Tito Ortiz, the other end of the fear spectrum. Tito was the UFC Light Heavyweight Champion from 2000 to 2003. The UFC is where two men go into a cage in the shape of an octagon and fight three or five, five minute rounds using fists, elbows, knees and feet to beat the other dude senseless, you can also use headlocks, arm bars and fun stuff like that and win the fight via the person tapping on your body or the mat before he loses consciousness or has a limb broken or dislocated joint, in short, good clean fun. Tito says that there are a lot of Latinos (as he calls them) that support Trump but are afraid to say it. It is so unfortunate that people are afraid to speak about their respective beliefs. Without dialog how can we learn from one another? Tito walks around with a MAGA hat on. Regarding President Trump saying criminals are coming over the border, A, he was right as I have shown, and B, Tito says that "it was just blown out of proportion." Everything that can be blown out of proportion has been and will be by the fake news. It will not stop after the election if President Trump wins. The fake news will continue to attack him to make Mike Pence look bad for being a part of the Trump Administration. The last thing they want is President Pence.

So what has President Trump and his administration done for people of color? I'll start with the easy one. He has delivered historically low Hispanic and Black unemployment numbers. The lowest in history for blacks,

Hispanics and Asians. One of the Black Panthers major goals in the 60's was full employment. President Trump delivered. The economy as a whole is at a 50 year low unemployment rate as mentioned in the introduction to this book. That means he has created opportunity for All Americans.

You've all heard of President Trump's tax cuts for the middle class.Nancy Pelosi stated that the $6,000 tax cut Americans got last year were crumbs. That is the word she used, "crumbs." She is so rich and out of touch she believes that $6,000 is crumbs. The median household income in 2017 in America was $62,000. This women has held political office for 27 years. She is the first female speaker of the house and she does not care about the American People one iota. The people that benefited the most from those crumbs were a majority people of color, relative to population. She then went on a rant lambasting President Trump for lowering taxes. Maybe she took too much medication that day, she is 80, aren't lower taxes good for the American People? "The paradoxical truth is that the tax rates are too high today and tax revenues are too low and the soundest way to raise revenues is in the long run is to cut rates now." John F. Kennedy.

Most people have not heard of The First Step Act. If you did hear about it, it was probably not from any of the fake news sources I've been exposing throughout this book. The First Step Act was signed into law in December, 2018. Before I go on let's keep in mind that 37 percent of the prison population is black, 22% is Hispanic and 32 percent white. These number vary but they are close enough for our purposes. Given the fact that white people are the majority in this country the first Step Act will have a larger impact on blacks and Hispanics, especially blacks who only make up 12.1 percent of the population but represent 37 percent of the prison population. The First Step Act enacted commonsense reforms to make our justice system fairer and help inmates successfully transition back into society. The act is designed for nonviolent offenders, leaning heavily towards people who are incarcerated because they have a drug problem. Over 16,000 inmates are enrolled in a drug treatment program offered as part of the robust drug treatment program managed by the Bureau of Prisons (BOP). We all know good people that have substance abuse problems. Some of these people are in our very own families or our friends of ours. Is it not better to get them help so that they can lead productive happy lives? Would that not be better than throwing a human being away for decades? A human being that only hurt himself. This legislation was long overdue. I have to ask. Why did no other president do it besides President Trump? The answer; they didn't care. The act also provided for sentencing relief for individuals who received mandatory minimum sentences prior to the Fair Sentencing Act of 2010. The act also authorized low-risk and elderly inmates to be transferred to home confinement when possible. This program will also save you, the tax payer money. Most sources say that the cost to incarcerate a prisoner for one year is $81,000. President Trump has also set aside 234 million for the Department of Justice to support reentry programs, inmate education, and occupational training programs. There is a further 78 million for the department of Labor to improve employment outcomes for formerly incarcerated adults and young adults. In 2019, the department of Education will provide 28 million for a Pell grant pilot program to help eligible incarcerated Americans pursue postsecondary education. These initiatives are intended to help reduce the rate of recidivism and offer prisoners the support they need for life after incarceration. You may be thinking the dollar amounts I've just mentioned are costing you more than the $81,000 per year to incarcerate a prisoner. If you take the 16,000 already mentioned in the program earlier and multiply it by $81,000 per year to incarcerate an individual you get $1,296,000,000. The cost of the programs mentioned above is 340 million. The First Step Act makes sense from a human standpoint as well as monetarily.

President Trump's commitment to H. B. C. U.'s is bigger and better than past administrations by far. According to Harry Marshall, the chief executive of the Thurgood Marshall College Fund, which represents 300,000 students who attend 47 publically funded H. B C. U.'s who was in the room for that meeting. He said: "We have seen some very positive gains as it relates to supporting our institutions. If you were there today, you heard the reaction from the audience, it was very respectful and cordial. You're not going to applaud if nothing is happening."[59] The article goes on to state that president Trump has increased funding by 14.3 percent. All this from the New York Times. I'm sure this bit of truth was way in the back of the paper.

In 2017, President Trump signed the Tax cuts and Jobs Act, which established Opportunity Zones to incentivize long term investments in low income communities across the country. These incentives offered capital gains tax relief to investors for new investment in designated opportunity Zones.

59   *The New York Times, Trump Focuses on Black Economic Gains and Support for Historically Black Colleges. By Annie Karni.*

Opportunity Zones are expected to spur $100 billion in private capital investment. Incentivizing investment in low income communities to create jobs and sustainable growth. This is what you get when you have a business man running the country. There are nearly 35 million Americans living in the designated Opportunity Zones. That is ten percent of the population of the U. S. This is what JFK said earlier, you lower taxes and businesses flourish. For a guy who is supposedly raciest he has done more than any other president to help minorities. One final point for this chapter.

Alveda King was a former member of the Georgia House of Representatives. She has an M. A. from Central Michigan University. She was a democrat from the 70's to about 1990. She has been a republican ever since. She is the niece of Dr. Martin Luther King Jr. Let's see what she has to say about President Trump and his alleged racism. Here's an article By Alveda King appearing in the Des Moines Register May,2 2019. Joe Biden is basing his entire candidacy on a discredited lie, trying to make President Trump seem like a racist so that Biden can present himself as some sort of "anti-racist" Candidate. That's the furthest thing from the truth. In the video announcing his candidacy for the Democratic presidential nomination, Biden cherry picked a partial quote from remarks the president made in the immediate aftermath of the Charlottesville riots, stripped of its context, and presented it as evidence that Trump had called neo Nazi's "fine people." That's a load of malarkey, and Biden knows it, President Trump also said that "neo Nazi's and white supremacists…. Should be condemned totally." The fine people he was referring to were the ordinary Americans, "on both sides," who felt passionately about a civic issue to demonstrate=peacefully-on behalf of their views. Unfortunately, Biden's accusations are perfectly in line with the Democratic Party's strategy of trying to inflame racial divisions, which conservative dynamo Candice Owens brilliantly exposed last month.

There are two central lies within Biden's launch video. The first is that Trump had a negative effect on the black community, and the second is that Biden could do better. In reality, though, President Trump has done more for Black Americans in just over two years than Biden has done in five decades as a public official. First and foremost the black unemployment rate is at its lowest point in history, due in large part to the president's efforts. Not only has the America First Agenda unleashed an historic economic boom, especially for blue color Americans, but Trump has also made it a priority to stop illegal immigration, which has disproportionally detrimental effects on the safety and wages of black workers. Over the past 27 months, black employment has increased by 1 million jobs, and this administration's policies boosting support for black owned small businesses and historically black colleges and universities will help us build on those gains for many years to come.

The other problem with Biden's claim that he can top President Trump as the best candidate for black America is that he'll have to run against his own record. The bipartisan FIRST STEP Act that Trump championed was, in large part, an effort to alleviate the mass black incarceration created by the 1994 omnibus crime bill that Biden has "no regrets" about writing. And what does Biden promise black voters, apart from unwarranted fear mongering about a "white supremacist" threat? He's just offering the same policies that have failed the black community for decades: high immigration, high taxes, and fake compassionate handouts that offer no way up for America's brothers and sisters. The distance between todays Democratic Party and the legacy of my uncle, Dr. Martin Luther King Jr., is wide and growing, and Biden has been the canary in the coal mine for years. Biden will not make good on the reconciliatory check prophesied by my uncle. In the 1970's Biden even opposed the use of busing to integrate public schools, and his instincts don't seem to have improved since then.

Remember his description of Barack Obama as "the first African American who is articulate and bright and clean and a nice looking guy." Or the time he told a black audience that republicans wanted to put them back in chains? Does anyone even remember it was the Republicans that broke the chains? What about when he said that you need "a slight Indian accent" to go to Dunkin Donuts or 7-11? He even assured us he wasn't joking about that one. Then there's Biden saying, "Poor kids are just as smart as white kids." Either he is a racist or these constant and ever increasing gaffes show that he has some form of dementia. Either way the dude is not fit to be president. Personally I think Homeboy's lost his natural mind and is a racist.

Ms. King then goes on to say she won't be voting for Biden and repeats that President Trump has presided over a record-breaking period of prosperity for the black community. Ms. King has repeated the above statements on social media as well as Fox News among others.

This brings us to true black patriot. A man who was lambasted by the Democratic Party and unfortunately his own people for indorsing President

Trump. His name is Vernon Jones. He is a member of the Georgia House of Representatives. His response to attacks by members of his own party for endorsing President Trump was quite succinct. When asked how he could possibly endorse President Trump his response was basically how could I not, citing President Trump's support for criminal justice reform and H. B. C. U.'s. He then went on to say "The way the Democratic Party has treated me this past week has made one thing clear: they are the bigots they claim to hate and I won't be silent about it." The strength of this man's convictions is admirable.

I remember the South Carolina debate in late February. I remember Biden suddenly peppering his verbiage with Y'all and other southern sounding statements. A wise man once told me beware of the man who pretends to be all things to all people. It's a bit like when you see these politicians like Biden and the other male candidates walking through a factory with their sleeves rolled up. It strikes me as a pathetic attempt to make people believe you are just like the people in the factory.

"I love when people call President Trump stupid…you mean the multi-billionaire who kicked every democrats butt, buried 16 career Republican politicians, and continues to make fools out of once reputable news organizations… You mean the guy who won the presidency? You mean the guy with the super model wife? You mean the guy whose words alone put a massive slow down on illegal border crossings? You mean the guy whose mere presence made the stock market smash its previous records? You mean the guy who created 1 million jobs his first 7 months in office? Are you sure you even know what it is you are resisting? Are you sure you back a party that enables the decimation of every core principle of Christianity? Are you sure you back a party that voted 100% against the abolition of slavery? Are you sure you really take a politician like Maxine Waters, seriously? Are you sure that you don't see anything wrong or peculiar about Hillary Clinton, a women involved in politics for the last 30 years having a net worth of $240 million? Are you sure you're not just having your opinion on hatred spewed by a crooked paid for media platform? Could you even tell me 5 things the Democratic Party has done to improve your day to day prosperity as a hard working American citizen? Probably not…Do you realize the debacle you are sending your children into once they become adults by continuing to support a political party that has done nothing for the poor except keep them poor, give them free abortions, and a few hundred bucks a month to keep food in the fridge? The prosperity and safety of its citizens is job one for your government. Get with the program. Everyone else has horribly failed you. Smarten up and take a position for your children. I promise you a country full of illegal immigrants, abortions, $15 an hour jobs, and non-gender specific people aren't going to make your country and life more prosperous. Rosie, Madonna, Katy Perry and Robert Deniro are not just like you. They don't have to live through the real world disparity of an average American.

Men don't hate women, white people don't hate black people and Donald Trump is not a racist. Stop allowing yourself to be brainwashed by a party that has continuously failed you. Be about your prosperity, your safety, your children, and an America first mindset. Dump these crooked politicians that have stunted your growth. Toughen up, take a stand, and act like a proud American.

See the spirit of Trump supporting freedom loving Americans and just imagine where we could be if everyone had the same priorities."
Clint Eastwood

Chapter 8

Tax Breaks and Trade Wars

It's a beautiful summer day in Southern California and I'm at the world famous Strand in Hermosa Beach. With me are two very large, strong men. They both own roofing companies and started in the trade when they were kids. One is a first generation Mexican, the other a first generation Italian. I say this because true to statistics, they are Democrats. One of the roofers says "whatcha been doin." I say, I've been writing a book about President Trump. They both growled a bit and one said "is it a pro Trump book?" I made sure the way to the door was clear and said "Yea, it is." They just looked at me like there was something wrong with me. I said "you both own your own companies right," they said "yea so." I said "you guys are incorporated right?" they said "yea, so." I said, "ya know Trump just dropped your corporate tax rate from 35 percent to 21 percent, how ya feel about Trump now?' They look at me and say "ohh, I like Trump now." Lunch was on them that day. This conversation took place a month after the tax break was announced and before it was time for them to do their taxes and hear the good news from their tax person. When you're running a company in a business as hard as the roofing business, you don't have a lot of time to watch the news. If you're watching the fake news, they will keep repeating the same lie over and over, President Trump gave tax breaks to his billionaire buddies. It's not just what the news says that can create a belief, it's what they omit.

You would be surprised how many small companies are incorporated, I was. If you have bought a home, your Real Estate agent may will have been incorporated, same with the person who did your loan. The person who appraised the house...same. Tons of tiny businesses are incorporated. In most states it takes one person to start a corporation. Some states require as many as three, but no more than that. The image I always had in my mind before I wrote a paper about corporations in college was that of a faceless, cold, uncaring behemoth concerned with making a profit at all costs. The reality is different for mom and pop corporations. So when President Trump cut the tax rate it benefitted your next door neighbor or a person a couple doors down or some person in you economic strata. United States small businesses employed 58 million people, or 47% of the private workforce in 2015. All economic data suggest that number is now larger.[60] So we know President Trump's tax cuts helped the little guys. What about the big bad corporations that Bernie and lots of other present/past Democratic presidential hopefuls like to demonize in an effort to get your vote. First of all, if you work for one of the 20% of private corporations that has a pension fund it is tied to Wall Street and big corporations. If you work in the public sector, teacher, law enforcement, postal worker etc., your pension is tied to Wall Street as well. It's the same if you have a mutual fund or simply own stocks. So these politicians saying they're going after Wall Street is nonsense. Taxing Wall Street's profits would be taxing your profits. That may sound strange coming from me given the spirit of this book, but it makes sense, think about it. The way to get the working person more money is to lower unemployment, this creates more competition for workers, this drives up wages. It's the oldest economic law, supply and demand. President Trump as a business man and not a career politician understands this simple law. Thus the lowering of the corporate tax rate and the increase in competition for workers, followed by higher wages. For the first time in decades the average workers' wages are going up faster than the guys at the top of the business.[61] Obama thought President Trump needed a magic wand. Who can forget his quote regarding the economy, when speaking of President Trump, "what's he gonna do, wave a magic wand." By lowering the corporate tax rate President Trump kept American jobs here, in the United States.

The corporate income tax (CIT) rate in China is 25%. A lower CIT rate is available for the following, qualified new high tech enterprises at 15%. Key software production enterprises at 10%. Qualified technology-advanced service enterprises at a CIT rate of 15%. Enterprises established in Zhuhai's Hengqin New Area are eligible for a CIT rate of 15%.[62] Is it any wonder that so many consumer goods are made in China? I remember going into

60   SBA.gov https://www.sba.gov?sites/default/files/advocacy/2018-Small-business-Profiles-US.pdf.

61   Wall Street Journal. Https://www.google.com/amp/s/www.wsj.com/amp/articles/rank-and file-workers-get-bigger-raises-11577442600.

62   PWC Worldwide TaxSummeries.https://taxsummeries.pwc.com/peoples-republic-of- xes-on-corporate-income. china/corporate/ta.

a Sketchers Shoe store, it was the size of a football field. Every shoe I picked up was made in China. I did not buy, not because I have anything against the Chinese people, I just like the Chinese people here in America better. Whether you are Christian or not, the way the Chinese government treats its people should not be supported by your dollars. We've already seen how they crack down on religion. Did you know they watch all 1.4 billion of their own people? They have set up facial recognition systems everywhere to shame jaywalkers, to forcing people to download apps that can access all the photos on their smartphones. They watch how their people shop online. Their tech companies are required to share user's information with the government. They stop pedestrians at random to check their phones. They track social media posts. They are building software to aggregate data about people-without their knowledge and flag those they consider dangerous or threatening.[63] If you think that can't happen here you haven't been reading my groovy quotes. It always starts somewhere else. It always starts with someone else. Here are two different headlines. Spy Agency NSA triples collection of U. S. phone records, Reuters, may 4th, 2018. NSA collecting phone records of millions of Verizon customers daily.[64] What does the NSA need with your phone records? So, why didn't any of our past Presidents say hey, we need to lower our corporate tax rate so the American corporations don't take their companies to China or elsewhere and American jobs with them? The Globalist want an economically depressed America so that Americans will cry out for handouts from the government. This gives the government more control. This leads to the end game of a One World Government. The math is real simple. The 35% American CIT rate prior to President Trump meant that the government in far too many instances got 35% of nothing as this that and the other corporation moved over seas. On top of all this China steals technology from the U. S. and any other country that has something they want.

It's not just China that has profited from our ridiculously high corporate tax rates. Check out the tag on some of the clothing you're wearing. It will not say made in the USA on it. The main reason for this is of course the former U. S. CIT rate. The second reason is slave wages being paid to the people of

---

63   Business insider.com. https://www.google.com/amp/s/www.businessinsider.com/how-china-is-watching-its=citizens-in-a-modern-survveillance-state-2018-4%3famp.

64   The Guardian, https://www.google.com/amp/s/amp/theguardian.com/world/2013/june/06/nas-phone-recoeds-verizon-court-order.

the nation's making the consumer goods. That boils down to greed. That's a bit hard to fix.

With the coronavirus or COVID-19 if you prefer, some disturbing realities have come to light. China is among the top producers of active pharmaceutical ingredients. Her are a few fun facts from The Pharma Letter: China produces 95% of U. S. imports of ibuprofen, 91% of U. S. imports of hydrocortisone, 70% of U. S. imports of acetaminophen, and 45% of Penicillin imports. In all 80% of the U. S. supply of antibiotics are made in China. This is the country that sickened 300,000 babies by feeding them milk powder that had been found to be adulterated with melamine, a toxic industrial compound.[65] These are not the people we want to be getting our lifesaving drugs from. The government of China is ideologically against our form of government. They wish to economically compete with us on a global stage. The article states that this has been going on for at least 20 years. With all this in mind do you think Obama, Bush and Clinton had the best interests and safety of the American people in mind when they did nothing about this? The article goes on to say that Congress is working on fixing this problem. A problem President Trump was already moving on before coronavirus.

Since we're on drugs, what has President Trump done about exorbitant prescription drug prices…A lot! In the 8 years before President Trumps inauguration-while Washington focused on government takeovers of healthcare rather than solving real world problems-prescription drug prices continued to climb by more than 3.5% year after year. Today prices for those drugs have seen a decline for the last 11 months. So what changed? The President changed, we got a new one. Here is what President Trump did: The FDA is now approving generic drugs at historically fast rates, generating savings for patients at 26 billion. President Trump has ended unacceptable pharmacy gag clauses, now pharmacists must tell patients about the best deals on medications they need. President Trump strengthened Medicare Part D. The administration finalized changes to Medicare's payment rate for certain drugs to lower expenses for seniors, as well as provided more tools to demystify out of pocked costs for beneficiaries. The result of these changes: prescription drug prices saw their largest year over year decline in more than 51 years.

---

65   Forbes, hyyps://www.google.com?amp/s/www.forbes.com/sites/yanzhonghuang/2014/17/16/the-2008-milk-scandle-revisited/amp.

President Trump has been demonized by the fake news regarding the "Trade War" with China. Fearmongering at its best. You've heard all this on the fake news ad nausea. Here are just a few headlines. American consumer, not China, are paying for Trump's trade tariffs, The New York Times. "Trump China Tariffs are Hurting U. S. Manufacturing." Bloomberg. I could go on and on. Here is something most of us did not learn in high school, (I didn't). Before the graduated income tax of 1914, the U. S. government got its money from tariffs and excise taxes. A heavy progressive or graduated income tax is Plank two of the Communist Manifesto. A so-called graduated "progressive" income tax is a violation of the principles of justice as it punishes those who are successful at creating wealth.[66] You may say things were cheaper back then before 1914's introduction of the income tax as we know it. Adjusted for inflation a battleship in 1900 cost the same as it costs today. The battleship technology at the time was cutting edge as it is now. From 1907 to 1909 Teddy Roosevelt sent 16 battleships and escort vessels around the world to demonstrate American Naval Power. The battleships and support craft were called The Great White Fleet. All this with tariff and excise taxes and no income tax. The trade imbalance President Trump had to fix was a result of generations of bad deals made by Globalist Presidents to weaken America. President Trump was being nice when he said past presidents were bad deal makers. The reality is they were Globalists. Tariffs are designed to Protect American workers. The fake news telling you the opposite is a lie. Was there some temporary pain for American Manufactures', yes? The pain was felt in the Midwest. Do you know that in the Midwest during this time President Trump's approval rating went up? The farmers were behind him nearly 100 percent. Being the true deal maker President Trump is he took the money from the tariffs and used it for temporary relief for the farmers. I say temporary because soon after the tariffs China started buying billions of tons of food from American Farmers. Let's think about this in common since terms. America has for decades been the number one exporter of food. We still are. How in the world could China have won a trade war with the U. S. We can get away with not buying a spatula for a buck at the Dollar Tree. How are they going to feed themselves without us? A trade war with China is like saying the Lion is going to battle the lamb. What we hear on the fake news is alarmism and doomsday fearmongering to make President Trump look bad. President Trump is undoing decades of Globalist handiwork and is being attacked daily by the Globalist controlled

66   *Graduated Income Tax/ Capitalism.org.*

media. Let's not forget that before the Coronavirus the stock market was breaking records the entire time President Trump has been in office. On February 12, 2002 it hit an all-time high of 19,551. It would probably be well above 30,000 had the coronavirus not hit. By comparison, the best Obama could manage was 19,804.[67] The stock market has never performed under any other president as it has under President Trump, the numbers don't lie. The Globalist controlled opinion pieces will try to dazzle you with grafts and economic trends and outside factors and blah, blah, blah. 29,551 under President Trump or 19,804 under Globalist Obama. President Trump created an environment that produced trillions of dollars of wealth for Americans with pensions, 401k's, or anyone with any money in whatever form, in the stock market.

---

67   *Nasdaq.*

Chapter 9

President Trump and
the Middle East

"There is no such thing as a Palestinian." Golda
Meir, Prime Minister of Israel, 1969-1974.

One of President Trump's campaign promises was to get our troops out of the Middle East. Like all his campaign promises he is keeping this promise as well. American forces have mostly pulled out of Syria and Iraq with huge troop reductions in Afghanistan. American troops are scheduled to be completely out of Afghanistan in July, 2021. It cannot be done overnight because the Middle East is a train wreck, made more so by western powers and Russia in their never ending hunger for oil and power. Israel is often on the front lines of this mess and being attacked by Muslim Countries made rich by the worlds thirst for oil. You will notice I said Muslim Countries. It is not the Arab world. That is a misnomer as is the term Palestinians. I remember reading an article in National Geographic about Iran. The writer said the first thing an Iranian will tell you is they are not Arab. They are Persian. The Egyptians, Afghanis, Iraqis, Persians, Turks and everyone else not from, or descended from people from the Arabian Peninsula, are not Arabs. The term "The war On Terror" that you saw in the news on a daily basis during the George W. Bush and Obama administrations is misleading as well. Terror is a method. You don't make war on a method. Call it what it is, the war on radical Islam. Now that you've identified the enemy, start ripping and gouging. This is war right? We are not going to earn the respect and fear of psychopaths with bon bons. President Trump dropped a bomb on an ISIS mountain hideout. The bomb he dropped was called the mother of all bombs. Although it is a conventional weapon it left a mushroom cloud that could be seen for twenty miles. The crater it leaves is a full mile in diameter. It was dropped on an ISIS cave network with tunnels that made it easy for ISIS fighters to appear, attack our troops and then melt back into the caves via the tunnels. That is how you get the respect and fear of psychopaths. This bomb dealt a serious blow to ISIS leadership and moral, but they are rebuilding. The situation is untenable as the United States 19 years in Afghanistan has shown. You cannot drop a bomb like that anywhere near a civilian population. You cannot tell who is ISIS or Al Qaeda or any other terrorist group from any other person on the street in Iraq, Syria or Afghanistan. You may have noticed that when film is shown of their fighters their faces are covered. How are you going to create peace with a weapon in your hand unless you are going to get ruthless and make total war? Keep in mind that the rules of engagement allow the enemy to engage first. So after American soldiers are shot at with AK47's, a stinger missile or blown up by an IED they can then fight back. This strategy has a serious flaw, what if the enemy has some good shooters among them. If they all shoot in unison and then run like cowards we then have dead U. S. Soldiers. You simply cannot win a war like that. It should be noted that they think the U.S. cowards as we launch drone strikes on them from 10,000 miles away. We need to be out of there as President Trump has said. I bit of very quick history to clarify today's Middle East as we know it. I hope to show that America or any other country is not going to bring peace to the region. I am writing this chapter because true to form, the fake news is lambasting President Trump for trying to get us out of the Middle East, stating it will create "instability." This is laughable statement as the Middle East has known no peace since Islam erupted from the sands of Arabia in the 7th century.

Let's start with the so called Palestinians. In 70 AD the Judeans (as the people of Israel were called at the time) revolted against Roman rule of their land. At that time Israel was the Roman Province of Judea. The Romans called their conquered territories provinces. Modern day France was called the Province of Gaul for instance. The emperor of the Roman Empire at the time, Vespasian, sent his son and successor Titus to quell the revolt. Titus utterly destroyed the second Jewish temple, and after the fall of Masada (a hilltop fortress in Israel) in AD 73 the rebellion was put down. In 135 AD the Jews rebelled yet again. This time it was Hadrian's turn to deal with the Jews. He instructed his generals to make total war. Men who fought, and their women and children were all killed. 500 of the rebellion's leaders were crucified. They then sold nearly, not all, of the survivors into slavery. This final insurrection so infuriated the Romans that they flushed every vestige of the Jews out of the land. Even the land itself was renamed. It was renamed Palestina, or Palestine.[68] Secular history and biblical references tell us beyond doubt that this was the land of the Jews. The bible tells us, as does secular history that though millions of Jews were dispersed after the second revolt against the Romans that a remnant always remained. So who owns the land? If we look at the land and the people on it from a historical perspective it is the land of the Jews. Here is what archaeologists have found regarding the first temple. It was called Solomon's temple, built circa 970 BC. In 1993, a tablet was found with the inscription by King Hazael of Aron-Damascus in about 825 BC, which indicated that his father, Hadad II was victorious in battle against the foot soldiers of the King of the House of David, against Jehosaphat, circa 860 BC. A second stone tablet, the Moabite Stone, revealed in 1995, contains 36 lines of Phoenician script that recounts the rebellion of king Mesha of Moab against King Jehoram of Isreal and King Jehosaphat of Judea (recorded in 2 Kings 3:5-27.[69] Secular and biblical historians tell us that Israel belonged to the Jews more than three thousand years ago. If we look at the land in terms of who fought and died for it in May 1948, the Israeli war of independence, it belongs to the Jews. Today we know the land as Israel, the only democracy in the Middle East. A nation that allows for representation of the people called Palestinians in the Israeli Knesset, the Israeli equivalent of the U. S. Congress. If we go a bit further back in time we will find no "Palestinians" in Israel. In 638 AD the Muslim Caliph Omar rested the land from the Christian Byzantine Empire. In 1099 the crusaders captured Jerusalem. The western rule of Jerusalem and the holy land ended in 1187 with the conquest of Salah-ad-Din, called Saladin by western peoples. Saladin by the way was what we call today a Kurd, (The Kurds are the largest ethnic group in the world without a country. They are 35 million strong. They too are trying to carve out a piece of Iraq and Syria as a homeland). During this entire time from Rome to Saladin there were Jews in the land. During the time of Muslim rule, Jews were still in the land, the remnant spoken of in the bible and secular history. The Jews were called people of the book by the Muslims as the Islamic faith recognized Jesus and Moses as prophets. The Jews had to endure a tax by virtue of being Jewish but were always tolerated in the land because of their knowledge in many sciences including medicine and in commerce. From 1229 to 1244 it was again in western hands as a result of the sixth crusade. From 1250

---

68   *Who Owns the Land, by Stanley Ellison.*

69   *https://www.ukapologetics.net/evidence.htm.*

to 1300 it was the Mamluks turn to conquer the land of modern day Israel and beyond. The Mamluks were Turkish slave warriors who rose up and became rulers. After the Mamluks it was the turn of The Ottoman Turks to rule the land until the end of WW1 when it was then divided by the French and English. It was at this point in time that Jews started migrating back to their land in increasingly large numbers. At no point during this entire period was there a distinct people called "Palestinians." "The Palestinian" people though invited by the Jews to fight alongside them and be part of a nation, left Israel during the 1948 war of independence. They were restricted to refugee camps in Jordan, Syria and Lebanon, by their Muslim brethren. Those that remained fled to the coast, away from the fighting in what we call the Gaza Strip. The Jews stayed and fought. Though heavily outnumbered in men and war material by Muslim forces from, Egypt, Syria, Transjordan, Yemen, Iraq, Lebanon and Saudi Arabia they prevailed. When I say heavily outnumbered in men and equipment that is an understatement. Here are the numbers: The Muslim Forces numbered 650,000, the Jews 45,000. The Jews had two rifles for every three men. With the holocaust still fresh in there memory, some of the Jews were attacking the enemy unarmed with sublime courage. If they fell while unarmed so be it, if the man with the rifle next to them fell they picked up the weapon and continued charging. The new/ancient nation now called Israel then endured the Sinai campaign in 1956, in this clash with Egypt, Jordan and Syria, the Soviets supplied the war material. Once again heavily outnumbered the Israeli's took ground. They could have taken Cairo but withdrew of their own accord. This war was fought due to the Egyptians cutting of Israeli access to the Suez Canal. Then there was the six day war of 1967. This time they were attacked by, Egypt, Jordan, Syria, Algeria and Kuwait. They were again heavily outnumbered and actually took land, including Jerusalem. Then there was the 1973 Yom Kippur war. This was a surprise attack during the Jewish Holiday led by Egypt and Syria. Again the Israeli's prevailed. There have been many military actions since then. The bible tells us the Jews were in Israel beginning about 3,200 years ago. Archeologists have found evidence from other cultures writing about the House of David. We have the Romans calling it Judea, we have the Catholic Church directing crusades to recapture the Holy Land from the infidel. The Israeli's have fought and died for the land. No matter how you look at it, it is the land of the Jews. The "Palestinians have been turned into martyrs by their Muslim brethren. Israel has been turned into the U.N.'s favorite nation to condemn and sanction. The Jews have been called racist by the fake news for their treatment of the "Palestinians." That is laughable as they share a common patriarch, Abraham. Abraham was the father of both Isaac of the Jews and Ishmael the father of the Arabs. Even the holy book of Islam called the Koran or Qur'an acknowledges Abraham as the patriarch of the Arabs. As we know, facts no longer matter to the fake news networks. What is so important about a tiny nation with no oil or mineral wealth that's making Islamic nations go nuts? Why does Iran promise over and over again to wipe Israel of the map? This is especially curious as they do not share a common border. There is no earthly or logical reason for the hatred of Israel. That leaves us with only one conclusion. The hatred is satanically inspired. When someone says something like that they are dismissed as a bible thumper or some other equally derogatory term. Christians and those of the Jewish faith believe that Satan was around since Adam and Eve were first deceived in the Garden of Eden. We do not believe he's on vacation. Dudes a hard worker. He never takes a day off. To further confound the current Middle East we have the schism of Islam itself. Again I'll be extremely brief on the origin of Islam.

Islam as a religion started circa 610 AD when Muhammad began receiving what Muslims considered divine revelations. It started in the western part of the Arabian Peninsula in Mecca and Medina. Muhammad in the early days was a caravan raider. We had a Muslim Cleric come to our church and I asked him about this, he did not deny it. After the death of Muhammad the religion spread extremely rapidly. Within 100 years the banner of Islam flew from Spain and Egypt in the west to the Punjab in the East, also encompassing modern day Syria, Iraq, Iran, and Afghanistan. The religion was spread by the sword. That is an undeniable fact. George W. Bush and Obama saying time and again that it is a religion of peace is fallacious. The crusades that are taught in school with the focus being on western crusades is only half the picture. In 711 Islamic Armies invaded Spain. They were there 700 years. They also crossed the Pyrenes Mountains and attacked France. They were met by Charles Martel, known as the hammer. It was Charles that stopped the expansion of Islam into Western Europe at that time. Southern and Eastern Europe including the Balkan States would be a Muslim targets as well. It should be noted that achievements in science, astronomy and medicine were made by the various Islamic Caliphates during medieval times. After the death of Muhammad Islam had what are called the four rightly guided Califs. The fourth, Ali, was a cousin of Muhammad's. He was assassinated by his fellow Muslims. This was the beginning of the schism we see in Islam today. The followers of Ali are Shiite, they make up 10 percent of

Islam, and the rest are Sunni. Iran has by far the most Shiites of any country. The Shiites and Sunnis have been at odds (euphemism for killing each other) for 1300 years. Bashar al-Assad is a Shiite belonging to the sect called Alawites. They get to drink wine while other Muslims are not supposed to. They also believe in reincarnation. It is the two main sects of Islam that are partly responsible for the current 11 year civil war in Syria, the current civil war in Yemen with Shia Iran on one side and Sunni Saudi Arabia on the other. The Yeminis' get to be in the middle. Regarding Syria, besides at least three different national factions, the Iranians, Russians and Turks are all involved. Meanwhile the 35 million Kurds in Syria and parts of Turkey and Iraq are desperately trying to carve out a country of their own. The Kurds are called the most numerous ethnic group without a country in the world. Then we have tiny Israel just trying to live in peace. On top of all that we had ISIS in the region before president Trump nearly obliterated them. They will be back. The fighting in the Middle East will continue. The United States or any other nation cannot stop it. Besides the Sunni/Shiite division, the Middle East has tribal blood feuds centuries old. The place is a train wreck. Since we know it cannot be fixed why we are there. We have been in Afghanistan for 19 years, nothing has changed but an estimated 8 trillion dollar cost, hundreds of dead Americans, thousands of dead Afghani's and more hatred from the Muslim world towards America. Prior to the U.S. being there, the Soviet Union was there for ten years. The soviets referred to the "conflict" in Afghanistan as their Viet Nam. I assure you the Soviets did not let the enemy shoot first and then allow their soldiers to engage. The soviets could not get what they wanted out of Afghanistan even with more ruthless tactics but short of total war. We will not either.

When President Trump ordered American soldiers out of Syria ABC showed the fake clip of explosions in Syria due to U. S. withdrawal. Crying out that President Trump is destabilizing the region. Those explosions were on a Kentucky gun range as discussed earlier. So first President Trump is wrong for leaving the Middle East. Then when President Trump and his advisor's ordered the killing of the rapist and murderer (Qasem Soleimani) responsible for the death of hundreds of Americans, all the fake news could talk about was how he was going to get us into a war with Iran. The inflammatory speech the fake news uses is laughable and constant. Think about it, the U. S. and Iran at war. Iran makes no long range bombers. They have no long range missiles capable of reaching us. How in the world could we go to war in Iran? Does the lion go to war with the lamb? The United States created

Star Wars in the 80's. I'm pretty positive if Iran had a missile capable of reaching our shores we could shoot it down with our tech from 30 years ago, what do you think we have now? Anything negative the Globalist controlled media can think of they will spew out live on CNN, MSNBC, ABC, CBS, NBC, or in print in TIME Magazine, The New York Times and the Washington Post, to name the biggest offenders in terms of viewership and circulation.

It was the same in December, 2017 when President Trump formally recognized Jerusalem as the capital of Israel and ordered the planning of the move of the U.S. Embassy to Jerusalem, yet another campaign promise made and kept. The Globalist news said it was going to cause "instability" in the region and make the Muslim nations angry. They said it was just a terrible idea. Clinton, George W. Bush and Obama all said they would do the same while running for office. They said this to pander for the evangelical vote. The difference is they never did it. They lied. The following link shows all three former presidents live on camera lying about what they were going to do.[70] By President Trump formally recognizing Jerusalem as the Capital of Israel he gave the nation more earthly credibility. This two state plan for Israel is not the answer. For one, the Muslims don't want some of Israel, they want it all. Secondly, God does not want it divided. "I will gather all the nations and bring them down to the valley of Jehoshaphat. Then I will enter into judgement with them there on behalf of My people and My inheritance, Israel, whom they have scattered among the nations; and they have divided up My land. Joel 3:2. Notice God says in capital letters His Land and My people. The land is not to be divided. Here is what the bible says about the nations and God's people. Now the Lord said to Abraham, "Go from your country and your kindred and your father's house to the land I will show you. And I will make of you a great nation, and I will bless you and make your name great, so that you will be a blessing. I will bless those who bless you, and him who dishonors you I will curse, and in you all the families of the earth shall be blessed." Genesis 12:1-3. Ezekial 37:21 tells us the following, then say to them, Thus says the lord God: Behold, I will take the people of Israel from the nations among which they have gone, and will gather them from all around, and bring them to their own land. Can there be any doubt he is speaking of the Jews? In Genesis 17:7-8 God

---

70 Realclearpolitics, https://www.realclearpolitics.com/video/2017/12/08/president_trump_tweets_montage_of_past_presidents_supporting_jerusalem_as_capital_of_israel.html.

says the following, and I will establish my covenant between you and me and your offspring after you throughout their generations for an everlasting covenant, to be God to you and to your offspring after you. And I will give to you and your offspring after you the land of your sojourning's, all the land of Canaan, for an everlasting possession, and I will be their God. If you look at this from a Judeo Christian reference point it is the land God gave to the Jews. If you look at it from a recent historical viewpoint in terms of who fought and died for it, it is the Jews land. If you want to look at it from a military perspective Israel has the most advanced military in the Middle East, history has shown us they are not going anywhere. There is always someone who wants to say isn't Jerusalem Islam's third most holy site? If it is it is curious that Jerusalem is never mentioned in the Koran. Not one time. By contrast Jerusalem is mentioned over 500 times in the bible. Because you hear Jerusalem is Islam's third most holy site over and over does not make it true.

We are now completely self-sufficient regarding oil. We are a net exporter. We don't need to send our soldiers to die in the Middle East to secure oil. It's interesting how the fake news lambasted President Trump for unleashing our domestic oil via an easing of job killing regulations. He's going to destroy the environment, and blah, blah, blah. We can produce oil here and stimulate our economy, and protect American soldiers, or we can send American soldiers at great economic cost to die, to "stabilize" countries that have never been stable. If you want to look at the situation from an environmental perspective fine. Does anybody really think the Saudis, Iranians, Iraqis' or anyone else that has oil is going to stop producing it? Would it not be better for the world's environment to produce it here where it's going to be used rather than ship it thousands of miles in oil tankers? I'm sure the extraction and refining of oil here is kinder to the environment than in any other country on earth. I realize that there is a low estimate of 1 trillion dollars' worth of rare earth minerals in Afghanistan. I know that is why Bush got us in Afghanistan and why Obama kept us there. President Trump has realized the futility of trying to police or bring peace to that region. He is also not in bed with the Globalists who want to rape and pillage Afghanistan of its natural resources. With that much wealth in the ground the Afghanistan people will figure a way to get it out, without our soldiers dying.

Chapter 9

President Trump and the Misogyny Smear

Sarah Elizabeth Sanders was President Trump's White House Press Secretary from July 26, 2017-July 1, 2019. She was preceded by Sean Spicer. I have respect and a genuine liking of Sean. Unfortunately, Sean appeared to wither under the assault of anti-Trump, fake journalists. So what did President Trump do? He found someone who would not appear to wither under constant attacks from less than pleasant people. President Trump, the man accused ad nausea of being misogynistic hired a woman for possibly the hardest and most important job …communicating to the people of the United States what he is really doing. Not only communicating for the president but defending him. Think about all the stress she endured every time it was time to talk to those rude, accusatory individuals. Sarah handled the job with verve, dignity, and a great deal more intelligence than her antagonists. On top of all that she came under personnel attack herself. That low class, inappropriate, so called comedy act, at the White House Correspondent Dinner by the foul mouthed Michelle Wolf, was just one example. President Trump comes from a business background, in that world you don't hire people because they fill a political box. You hire them to do a job because they are the best human being to get it done. President Trump hired a woman. To me this sounds like a very open minded, pragmatic person. Not a Misogynist. But again, the Globalist Media must paint President Trump as anti-women in a desperate attempt to take votes away from him.

Do you know who appointed the first women to successfully run a presidential campaign? President Trump. Her name is Kellyanne Conway. She is razor sharp. These fake news media so called journalists are simply out of their league when matching their dim wits against Sarah and Kellyanne.

It should be noted that President Trump appointed Kellyanne Conway before he was accused of misogyny. Kellyanne is now the Counselor to the President. It sure looks to me like he has a lot of faith in these two women. Sarah to speak up for him against the hyenas and Kellyanne to give him solid advice. If you have ever heard Kellyanne speak it doesn't take long for you to come to the conclusion that this is one sharp human being...who happens to be female.

Who did President Trump appoint as the U. S. ambassador to the UN? Nikki Haley. Her given name is Nimrata Randhawa, she is of Indian descent. I'm sure that most of you reading this book can't name more than a few U. S. Ambassadors to the UN. I know I can't. My point is that Trump didn't appoint her because it is a high profile position. He didn't appoint her because she would make him look good. The UN ambassador is not someone you see in the news. So why a woman like Nikki? Because she is the best person for the job. Here are a few reasons why. Her parents were immigrants form the Punjab region of India. Her father was formerly a professor of agriculture and her mother an attorney. Imagine the dinner table conversations and how much she learned as a child of immigrants. How much knowledge was she able to bring to her job as our UN ambassador? Immigrants are hard to fool when you start telling them how things work in other countries, they have been there, they know. Nikki is the first woman to have served as governor of South Carolina and also the first Sikh governor of a U. S. state. I guess President Trump didn't know that she was Indian and a Sikh because the fake news will tell you he's a raciest, constantly. Here is yet another example of President Trump appointing someone to a job based solely on their merits. Not if they are male or female. Again, businesses run best when the best person is in the proper job, so do countries. Here is a list of yet more women appointed by President Trump to important positions. These women were not appointed in an election year to pander for the female vote. The majority of these women were appointed in the first year of President Trump's administration.

Elaine Chao is the current Transportation Secretary. She also happens to be an immigrant from Taiwan.

Betty DeVos is the current Department of Education secretary. Here again is another position that you don't hear much about in the news. She is not window dressing.

Gina Haspel is the first female CIA Director. She is not a member of the CFR. In my mind that is far more important than the fact that she is a woman, in President Trump's mind I believe, as well.

Javita Carranza, Treasurer of the U. S., also a minority and first generation Mexican American.

Neomi Rao, Regulation Czar, also a minority and daughter of parents from India.

Seema Verma, Administrator of the centers for Medicare and Medicaid services. She is also a minority.

Heather Brand, Associate Attorney General.

Kelly Sadler, Director of Surrogate and Coalitions outreach.

Mercedes Schlapp, Senior communications Advisor. She is also first generation Cuban whose father was once a political prisoner of Fidel Castro.

Hope Hicks, Communications director.

Jessica Ditto, Deputy Director of Communications.

Dina Powell, Deputy National Security Advisor.

Some of the above women have left their posts of their own accord. Some were let go. Some left and have now come back. Some were replaced by other women and some were replaced by men. President Trump is interested in the best human being for any given job. It is that simple. As I write this chapter we are in the midst of Covid-19. President Trump appointed Dr. Deborah Birx as the response coordinator for the White House Coronavirus task Force.

These women that made all these baseless claims accusing President Trump of anything they could think of were all, all proven false. One of the false accusations was made by a porn star whose attorney (Michael Avenatti) is now in prison for extortion. When he couldn't get any money from President Trump he thought he'd extort millions from Nike. Thus the prison term.

The interesting thing about this story is the incredible amount of coverage the fake news gave these two crooks. As soon as Avenatti was accused of extortion the Globalist news completely ignored him and his porn star client. They then went in search of the next bit of fiction they could spin in yet another desperate attempt to paint President Trump in a bad light and thus cost him votes. While I'm on these baseless claims diatribe, have you ever noticed how many "unnamed sources" there are and how constantly a new smear against President Trump starts with: according to unnamed sources. When you hear that phrase you are being lied to. I think that now a days the majority of men are not caught up in the whole me Tarzan you Jane thing. I'm quite sure that most women don't feel somehow inferior. The Globalists are behind the times. Then again, they are desperate.

Chapter 10

The Democratic Candidates

Some of these men and women have already dropped out of the race. I'm just having a little fun with the ones that are gone.

Beto O'Rourke, Real Name: Robert Francis O'Rourke.

He goes by Beto to pander to the large Hispanic population of Texas. Beto was heard to say on the Democratic debate stage "hell yes, will take your AR15's". Beto may have thought he actually had a chance at the Democratic nomination. I can't be sure as I've never been able to understand nut jobs. I am sure he was pandering to the Globalists because they know it is imperative to their New World Order (George H. W. Bush's words) to take Americans guns. Here's the problem with taking Americans guns away, especially in a state like Texas and especially those types of guns. The Americans that have AR15's and any other guns feel quite strongly about their second amendment rights. Many of these women and men are former soldiers who know how to use them. They also know tactics. They are not going to give you their guns. How then are you going to "take" them? Listen up Beto, I'm going to teach you about United States law. Have you ever heard of Posse Comitatus? It's only been around since 1878. It says quite clearly that the government cannot use the United States armed forces to police civilians, so Beto, who is going to take away the guns of former United States soldiers, some of whom where members of various United States special forces. You're not going to do it. The law states the National Guard could intervene. Do you think a bunch of once a month part-timers are going to even try to follow and order to do so? Don't be ridicules. Have you ever heard of the three percent? It is estimated that three percent of American Patriots would take up arms against the government to protect their constitutional rights. That's 9 million plus Americans. One other thing, stop rolling up your sleeves like you're a regular guy. We know you're from a political family. Lastly, stop the angry shacking of your arms and hands when you speak, it's reminiscent of Hitler.

Kamala Harris

The crocodile tears she shed for families struggling because they could not buy cheap Chinese goods was pathetic. There are millions of Americans who know about the one million plus Uighurs held by the Chinese government in reeducation camps. The camps are not only for reeducation they are also work camps. An Australian Target store did an independent study to determine which goods are made by the Uighurs. Since China is the least transparent of countries I wish them luck. Incidentally the Muslim Religion has been all but wiped out in China with Christianity not far behind. I guess slave labor is not as important to Kamala as cheap goods.

Elisabeth Warren

Besides her "I have a plan for that", she has a huge problem recognized early by her handlers, her voice. It comes off weak. Perception is huge, unfortunately, maybe bigger then the truth. If our history of elected officials is the yardstick then perception is indeed bigger than truth. After the first debate her handlers recognized the problem of her voice and had her making statements like "I'm not afraid" and "I'll fight". The problem is, she is still using the same voice to make those statements (Hillary did not have that problem.) No one can see her standing up at the negotiation table with Putin, Rocket Man, or the two Iranian nut cases. Her Pocahontas story didn't help as well. Elizabeth is wasting her time.

Gabbard, Tulsi is long gone from the race. She did have something interesting to say. She said the L. A. Times and CNN were despicable. I like Tulsi. Her ongoing battle with Hillary is interesting to behold and a sign of the fragmentation of the Democratic Party.

Klobuchar

I have nothing against her other than her politics. I mean this in the nicest way. She is just not perceived as presidential, whatever that intangible presidential thing is, she does not have it.

Steyer

At the South Carolina debate he was invisible. The whole "I'll declare a climate emergency my first day as president" is not going to do it, given the fact that he made tons of money in coal just a few short years ago pretty much sinks his boat. Perhaps he doesn't realize that people are now doing internet searches on candidates. He is wasting his time. Maybe he doesn't realize that tattoos are temporary and the net is forever.

Buttigieg

He will not get the Black vote. It just won't happen. Since the black vote is necessary to win the Democratic nomination he is wasting his time. His youth and being a smallish town mayor does not help. He is slick. I'll give him that.

Bloomberg

Bloomberg is running for president because his Globalist bodies know that Biden may not have the steam to get the job done. Bloomberg is a CFR member and allegedly a Bilderberger attendee. He will not get the Black vote. His racist policies and remarks while mayor of New York are now front and center thanks to his fellow democrats. He might have had a chance to win the democratic nomination due to the tremendous amount of money he is throwing into his candidacy had his fellow democrats not sunk his boat. I believe that Bloomberg has not read the prevailing political winds. Judging by Sanders grass roots support on an anti-Billionaire platform, the fact that he is perceived as buying the nomination is not going to fly. Bloomberg will get some delegates. That is very important. You'll see why shortly. His attacks on President Trump on his campaign ads are in line with his Globalist agenda.

Biden

Poor Joe. Sleepy Joe has three problems, here they are in order of increasing magnitude. His constant gaffs are making him appear (rightly so I believe) that he's not all there. His hubris and reckless braggadocio caught on camera at the CFR regarding Ukraine will certainly be shown on President Trump's campaign ads. His biggest problem is President Trump. President Trump is in Biden's head, so much so that he changed the way he spoke at the last two Presidential Debates. Because of President Trump referring to him as Sleepy Joe, Biden now says everything with too much vigor. It comes off as disingenuous. He has the Fake news behind him which is huge. He also has the Globalist controlled democratic machine behind him, also huge. Sanders was sandbagged once against Hillary, it will happen on behalf of Biden this time. On top of his gaffs, Ukraine and the psych job President Trump has done on him. It seems that he feels he shouldn't have to be doing all this campaign stuff. It's as though he feels it's his turn. He has been a loyal servant to the powers that be and I believe it vexes him that he's got to go through all this campaigning rigmarole. It is amazing to me that someone with all the recent corruption and past (how do I say this) really dumb quotes, is going to be the Globalists best chance…mindboggling! On top of all that he caught constantly lying, here are two examples: "I went to law school on a full academic scholarship, the only one in my class who had a full academic scholarship." He also claimed he graduated with three degrees and at the top of his class. He graduated with two degrees and number 76 out of 85 students at his law school.

On an interview with Charlamagne tha God on The Breakfast club, Biden says "Well, I tell you what, if you have a problem figuring out if you're for me or Trump, then you ain't black." Interesting verbiage, I like the way he peppers his speech with what he thinks is black speak, that is a form of lying. The blatant lie was what he said at the end of the interview. Biden says "The NAACP has endorsed him every time I've run." The NAACP quickly came out and said we've never endorsed him or anyone else. This from NAACP President Derrick Johnson. So we know Joe Biden is a liar or he just can't remember stuff.

Sanders

I believe he should win the Democratic nomination. I do not think he will get the Democratic nomination. I think he will be robed as he was in 2016. The Globalists do not want him. Though his name appears on CFR rosters he is not in the inner circle. When he asked then Federal Reserve Chairman Ben Bernanke about congressional oversight of the Fed he sealed his fate. He is unacceptable to the Globalists as was candidate Trump. Trump made it to the Whitehouse because he is smarter and probably had his people making sure he was not robbed. He also had a much better message. Sanders is waking up. He is starting to hit back at the Globalist media that is trying to tank him. I just don't think that he has the necessary tools and energy to fight them off.

I have an unsettling premonition that by hook and crook Biden well wind up being the Democratic nominee. That is a sad commentary on our Constitutional Republic. If Sanders can fight off the fake news, the democratic machine and overcome his own party's fraud, it will be Sanders. If that sounds crazy to you let's take a quick look back at recent history.

When Al Core walked onto the stage for his movie, An Inconvenient Truth, he says, Hi, I'm Al Gore, I used to be president." He is referring to the 2000 presidential race between himself and George W. Bush. The race came down to Florida. Whomever won that state would be President. It was initially announced that Gore had won. He was the President, soon thereafter it was announced that a recount was being done. The next day it was announced that Bush had won. Jeb Bush was the Governor of Florida at the time, I'll let you draw your own conclusions. There was a lot of talk of fraud. That talk was soon silenced. The person who was not screaming fraud was none other than Gore. Why did he not scream as loudly as his supporters? He did not scream bloody murder because he is a part of the same hypocrisy. The establishment can't have the herd doubting the veracity of presidential elections. If the herd were to rise up, all the Globalists might be thrown out. CFR member Al Gore was out played by CFR family member and Bonesmen George W. Bush. A quick word on Skull and Bones. It was founded in 1832 at Yale University, membership is for life, only 15 members are accepted a year. They are very serious about the life part. One of John Kerry's responses to being asked about Skull and bones was "what are you trying to do, get rid of me"? When George W. was asked about it he replied "In my senior year I joined Skull and Bones, a secret society; so secret I can't say anymore. John Kerry who ran against George W in the 2004 election was asked again what it meant that two Bonesmen were running against one another for President he replied "Not much, because it's a secret. Skull and Bones has the same goal in mind as the CFR and the Trilateral Commission, a New World Order, with them in charge. Skull and Bones is tiny but more exclusive, most of it's members are CFR members as well. Here are some notable members: Prescott Bush, both Bush Presidents. President William Taft, He was also a Supreme Court Chief Justice., Supreme Court Justices, Morrison R. Waite and Potter Stewart, James Jesus Angleton, "mother of the CIA, Henry Stimson, secretary of War (mentioned earlier), Henry Luce, (mentioned Earlier) founder and Publisher of Time, Life Sports Illustrated and Fortune magazines; Stephen A Schwarzman, founder of Blackstone Group. Lastly for this list anyway, Austan Goolsbee, Chairman of Economic Advisors for Obama. We have to have a quick word on one other member, McGeorge Bundy. He was called one of JFK's wise men. It was Bundy who was heavily responsible for the evolution of the Vietnam War. It seems to me that a society that wields this much power and has secrecy rules upon pain of death is probably not good for Americans. The fact that they are interlocked with the CFR and Trilateral Commission and let the two Bush boys in leads me to believe they are probably not great from America.

Regarding the Presidential election, I think the Globalists will do what they did to get Wilson elected. They will run a third party moderate candidate to take votes away from President Trump (remember Teddy's Bull Moose Party from the chapter on the Fed). I think the third party candidate will have a platform similar to President Trump's. It's unfortunate that we as citizens forget or are not taught our true history in school. I promise the Globalists have not forgot how they got Wilson elected so he could give them control of our money.

So, how would the nomination be stolen from Bernie, Delegates. Delegates that are pledged to a candidate that drops out don't just disappear. They are "given" to someone. They are typically given to the candidate that the withdrawn candidate indorses. The crazy thing is the delegates do not have to give them to the candidate that the dropout/withdrawn candidate designates. The delegates have a lot of power and are typically under the sway of their national party. In this case the DNC (Democratic National Committee). The DNC coordinates strategy and more importantly money. The DNC strategizes and coordinates races all over the country for local, state and national office. If you are Butigiege and you want to be a congressman you will do as you are told and indorse BIden. If you are Klobuchar and want the help of the DNC for re-election you will do as you are told and indorse Biden. Butigiege had 27 delegates and Klobuchar all of 8. We know these two are ambitious otherwise they would not have run for president. They will not make a fuss. So what is a delegate? A delegate can be a volunteer, a party char (much more likely) or even an interested citizen. They are supposed to use their conscience and reflect the sentiments of those who elected them. The bad news is they don't have to. This is a giant problem.

This is what Bernie is going to have to overcome. But wait there's more! We still have CFR member Bloomberg in the race as well as Warren. Warren is going to fail. Knowing what you know, who do you think will get her delegates? I think Bloomberg's ego causes him to think he could win, that and his money. I am quite sure that he will get some delegates and when his path to defeat is clear he will indorse Biden and Biden will receive his delegates. I almost feel sorry for Sanders. He going to live 2016 all over again. There is some good that can come out of it. Sanders at 78 may realize he is not going to live forever and will never be President. I am hoping he goes on a verbal rampage and tells anyone who will listen that President trump is right, Washington is a swamp. He did say in the March 15th debate that the news is controlled by billionaires.

Chapter 11

Coronavirus

Coronavirus also known as COVID-19 did not come from a fresh meat market in Wuhan China. It came from a lab in Wuhan China. The reason it is called COVID-19 is because that it is the strain of COVID we are dealing with, for instance SARS was COVID-2. SARS 1 is only a decade old. For the virus to jump from animals to humans can take up to 800 years. It certainly did not happen in a decade. This and the following information comes from Dr. Judy Mikovits. Here is where things get really interesting. Up until a few days ago she could be seen on YouTube under Plandemic, speaking on this subject. It went viral. In just a few days it had a couple million views. I just now tried to re access it but YouTube took it down…again. When I went to the website this is what I saw; this video has been removed for violating You Tube's Community Guidelines. Wow! Censorship, just like they have in China, Iran and North Korea. I am aware that there is a huge smear campaign against this women. I saw many sites dismissing her as another conspiracy theorist. Many of the sites say she is anti-vaccine. She states very clearly and unmistakably that she is not anti-vaccine. The fact that the video has been censored lends it credibility in my eyes, especially because she is not the only one saying things of this nature. There is also documentation from the Rockefeller Foundation predating some of what Dr. Wikovits' says in the interview. I'll share that link later, hopefully it will still be accessible. I was able to see the Wilkovits' interview before censorship and thought her to be credible and factual. In the video she states that five years ago she was the victim of an unlawful search of her home, no warrant, by the FBI. She was then put under a gag order for five years. She states that if she spoke on the subject during those five years the FBI would find more evidence against her. Yes, it sounds nuts to me as well. Unfortunately I was only able to view the video once so what I'm about to share are the things I remember clearly, I will leave out what I don't remember clearly in the interest of factualism. The good news is, is that a documentary is coming out on the subject in July of 2020. In the video, Dr. Mikovits goes on to say that Anthony Fauci was culpable in delaying proper recognition of HIV. She states that huge bribes were paid. She states that a lab in North Carolina was instrumental in the development of the Coronavirus we see today. The virus was then taken to China. Dr. Mikovits stops short of saying that the virus was purposely released, however she is quite clear in saying that yes it did come from the lab in Wuhan. As of this writing the Department of Health and Human Services is being sued by Judicial Watch to obtain communications between Anthony Fauci, Clifford Lane, Deputy Director of Clinical Research of Allergy and Infectious Deseases, and the WHO. She speaks of universities now getting 16 times as many patents as they did in the 1980's. She is speaking of biological patents. She goes on to say that Coronavirus deaths are being vastly over reported because if a hospital says the death was suspected of being from Coronavirus the hospital would get $13,000 from Medicare. If the death occurred while the patient was on a ventilator and the cause of death was listed as coronavirus the amount paid by Medicare is $39,000. I gave that a moment's thought as to why a Dr. would do something like that. I came up with two reasons. The first reason could be that a doctor knows that hospitals are constantly short of money. With more money more good can be done. The second reason is fear. If caring doctors know that a high death toll will frighten people to stay home perhaps that would save lives by slowing the spread. I am also told that the CDC has directed hospitals to tell doctors that if the cause of death is suspected to be Coronavirus they are to list the death as Coronavirus. I am not in any way blaming doctors. There is much more in the video but It seems that we will all have to wait until July. She did recently have a book published on the subject called: Plague of Corruption, Restoring Faith in the Promise of Science. It is a bestseller. Unfortunately I have not had the time to pick it up.

Recently a very disturbing video came my way from a friend at the gym. These are the Rockefeller foundation links regarding pandemics I mentioned earlier. One link is a video done by a very passionate man by the name of Harry Vox. He is an Investigative Journalist. The interview is from 2014. Here is the link.[71] Documentation link,[72] Please pay special attention to page 18.

---

71   https://theferalirishman.blogspot.com/2020/04/this-is-quite-interesting-12minute.html?m=1.

72   https://www.nommeradio.ee/meedia/pdf/rrs/Rockefeller%20Foundation.pdf.

The above video and supporting documentation describe how the Globalists can use/create pandemics to further their goal of a One World Government. Again, population control has long been on their agenda.

We know from our previous reading that the U.N. is a globalist organization. We know that the WHO is corrupt and has long been under Chinese influence. We also know that due to the WHO's handling of Coronavirus, or lack thereof, that President Trump pulled American funding from the WHO. The timing of this pandemic is interesting. We have a President up for reelection that has been tougher on China than any president since CFR member Nixon opened China in the early 70's (after David Rockefeller and Henry Kissinger met with Chinese Premier Zhou Enlai in 1972). Rockefeller was the first banker to meet a Chinese leader since China became communist in 1949. The Rockefeller family has ties to China going back 100 years.[73] The Rockefeller Family has invested hundreds of millions of dollars in China over the past century. In 1921 the family founded the Peking Union Medical College with a budget of 8 million dollars. That's 1921 money. It stands to reason that China does not want Trump in the Whitehouse. The Rockefeller Family certainly doesn't. Presidents that are up for reelection lose for two reasons, an unpopular war or an economy in shambles. Neither of those scenarios apply to the Trump Administration. Quite the opposite in fact. I believe it is probable that this virus did not get out of the Wuhan lab by accident. Communist China's entire history is one of disdain for the lives of their own people. One hundred thousand dead countrymen mean nothing to the Chinese Communist Party, history has, and continues to show us that sad fact. Regarding the CCP (Chinese Communist Party), we should not buy from China. Since most commerce in China is owned by the state, when you buy from China you are supporting a regime against everything that America stands for. The answer is simple, don't buy from China. On Wednesday May 6, 2020, President Trump stated that this virus has killed more Americans than Pearl Harbor and 911 combined. If Coronavirus was not enough, they constantly manipulate their currency, steal our technology and treat their people with utter disdain for their humanity. Are we going to reward the CCP by buying their goods?

The way some governors are stomping on our rights is disturbing to say the least. When 6,000 doctors are saying Hydroxychloroquine works and

73   https://chinaplus.cri.cn/news/china/9.20170321/1789.html.

President Trump says he takes it, I think it's safe to say that unless you have underlying health issues that it's ok to come out and play. Especially given the fact that we know sunlight kills the virus. It is interesting to note that the mass media painted HCQ as a dangerous drug. HCQ has been around for 65 years. Millions of prescriptions a year were written for it prior to Coronavirus. Facts never stand in the way of the main stream media. Scientists have told us that it is less transmittable outdoors with proper distancing, yet governors like Gavin Newsom of California kept beaches closed long after what you just read became public knowledge. He's also trying to give 75 million of tax payer money to illegal immigrants. You can't make this stuff up. Michigan Gov. Democrat Gretchen Whitmer is being sued by her own state legislature for her government overreach. By Comparison many Republican Governors have already opened up there states. People need to get back to work.

Obama, Hillary Clinton and Obama's former Attorney General Eric Holder are all behind Michelle Obama's vote from home initiative. True to form the Globalists never let a crisis go to waste. The narrative goes like this, people should not have to risk their health to participate in democracy. Never mind that voting from home via the mail has a proven track record of fraud. The Globalists are coming at President Trump on all fronts. In 2017 Judicial Watch sued California and L. A. County to force a cleanup after finding 1.6 million inactive voters on California voting rolls. The investigation found that L. A. County had more voter registrations on its rolls than actual voting age citizens in the county. California was a state that Hillary won. North Carolina had one million inactive voters on its rolls. Ohio, Maryland, Kentucky, Iowa and Indiana all had similar problems. So with all of this in mind do we really need more windows of fraud opened?

I believe Anthony Fauci to be highly suspect. I believe by the time this book is out in late September he will be ousted by President Trump. Dr. William Scott Magill is the Executive Director of Veterans in Defense of Liberty. He served in the U. S. Army Medical Corps from 1981-1988. He tells us the following: It's time to seriously question everything we know about the physical and the cultural virus. H goes on to state that Fauci a longtime bureaucrat paid 3.7 million to the Wuhan laboratory for corona-virus development after the U. S. declared a moratorium on such funding. Fauci is joined at the hip with Bill Gates, paid for the scam VA study at the University of Virginia and has been on the payroll of the Clinton Foundation for years. He is responsible for the death of thousands of Americans by leading opposition to a drug regimen that is at least 91% effective in curing SARS-CoV2 infections-thereby violating his Oath-"first do no harm"-and his responsibility to America and Americans. Now he gleefully flaunts the success of Remdesivir, which was initially developed in 2016 to fight Ebola and made by Gilead Sciences as the cure for COVID-19. He goes on to state that Fauci has close ties to Tedros Adhanom Ghebreyesus, the director of WHO. He states that China owns the patent on Remdesivir. He goes on to state that Gilead Sciences is partnered with Wuxi AppTec which is owned by CFR member George Soros. He states Soros is also an investor in Gilead Sciences. He states that the FDA (the same organization that approved cancer causing Aspartame, with help from CFR member Donald Rumsfeld) tried to limit Hydroxychloroquine to hospital use where the window of maximum effect has passed. He states the virus is 99.6% survivable without underlying medical conditions. He then speaks of our loss of liberty as a result of the lockdown. He then askes some penetrating questions. Why is Hydroxychloroquine which is 91% successful in curing COVID-19 not being used early before hospitalization because of the FDA? It is a fraction of the cost of Remdesivir. Since sound science and accurate data are essential for combating any pandemic, why have Dr. Brix and the federal government (CDC) directed doctors to classify the cause of death on the death certificate to grossly inflate the COVID-19 death rate even if they only "assume" COVID-19; while other primary causes of death exist?[74][75]

So here is another prominent doctor supporting what Dr. Mikovits has said. Here is one more doctor saying much the same thing and siting some extremely exciting science in the Coronavirus fight. This just came out 7/2/2020, it is from a Texas doctor by the name of Richard Bartlett. He says that Taiwan a country of 25 million has had a total of 7 Coronavirus deaths. Japan a country of 121 million has had less than 1,000 Coronavirus deaths, Singapore a country of 5.6 million has had 12 deaths. They did not achieve these low numbers by social distancing, nor did they achieve these low numbers by using HCQ, though he agrees it works in the early stages. Japan and these other countries used a common inhaled steroid that 20 million Americans of all ages have used for 20 years. He goes on to say its payable by most insurance companies and that 51 peer reviewed papers supporting

74   Tony Fauci and the Trojan horse of tyranny,
75   *https://www.wnd.com/2020/05tony-fauci-trojan-horse-tyranny/*

his findings are on the way out and that Senator Ted Cruz is now aware. Dr. Bartlett also wonders aloud why we are following what the WHO and China's practices are. He wonders aloud why we are telling people don't go to the hospital until you are very sick when we should be giving them HCQ or the inhaler early. He goes on to say he believes there is an agenda. The video is 31 minutes long. Here is the info and link:[76]

I think it is only a matter of time before Fauci is ousted by President Trump. There are thousands of Doctors saying that Hydroxychloroquine works, that fresh air is good and that deaths from COVID-19 are vastly over reported. Senator Rand Paul (Rep) Kentucky is a medical doctor. After doing his homework and reading recently compiled data that is widely available this is what he had to say March 13, 2020: People aged 0-18 have a 1/100[th of] one percent chance of dying from COVID-19, people aged 18-45 about the same. He goes on to state that Fauci is not the end all when it comes to this virus. There are tons of Doctors coming out against Fauci and the shutting down of our economy. Some well-respected prominent Doctors such as David Samadi have publicly stated Fauci is plain wrong and have offered President Trump their services.[77]

The fake news is constantly accusing President Trump of not acting swiftly enough to combat this virus. I am inserting a timeline so that when the history books are written and they claim something different there will be an additional source telling the truth. The following dates and information are a matter of public record (for now) and come to us from 1600 Daily. On January 29th President Trump formed a Coronavirus task Force when there were just a handful of cases in the U. S. The New York Times warned its readers to "beware the pandemic panic." Two days later President Trump restricted travel from China. Democratic leaders called the ban "xenophobic" and unnecessary. The Washington Post published a piece that day: "How our brains make coronavirus seem scarier than it is." On February 24, President Trump requested 2.5 billion from Congress in emergency funds to fight the virus. That same day, the WHO insisted Coronavirus was not a pandemic-and chillingly praised China's government for getting it under control. In an oval office address on March 11, President Trump spoke about the travel restrictions from Europe. Speaker Nancy Pelosi

---

76   *Dr. Richard Bartlett | ACWT interview 7.2.2020, https;//m.youtube.com/watch?v=eDSDdwN2Xcg*
77   *Bizpacreview.com, July 3, 2020.*

joined the media and other Democrats in questioning the action. "Well see whether it's worth the trouble." The Trump Administration negotiated with Congress later in March to get immediate relief for working Americans through the bipartisan CARES Act. Speaker Pelosi and House Democrats stalled the Senate bill with their own list of demands-filled with partisan items that had nothing to do with Coronavirus. So first President Trump acted too fast and then he didn't act fast enough. All the while the fake news is busily repeating what top democrats say and ignoring the hypocrisy that they themselves are a part of.

As of July 1, 2020 the science proving HCQ's ability to treat Coronavirus in its early stages is undeniable. I am seeing more and more YouTube videos where doctors with peer reviewed papers advocating the use of HCQ are being taken off YouTube. You've gotta ask yourself why. If Fauci was really doing his job shouldn't he have read these peer reviewed papers?

Reliable News Sources

One America News Network: OANN is based in San Diego California. It is on 24/7. It states that it gives you four times the news in the same time as other networks. I believe it to be more like twice that amount, they are being modest. On this station you will see Trump rallies and interviews that the fake news will never show you. They will also run specials on things like the Biden Quid Pro Quo in Ukraine and Globalist CFR member George Soros claiming on camera he is the nearest thing to God on earth and stating he does not believe in God. They have two commentators that are absolutely great, Liz Wheeler and Graham Ledger. During commercial breaks they will give you a different constitutional amendment, a nice refresher course, brief and concise. By brief I mean 90 seconds at most. They are also found of showing clips of politicians and the fake news saying one thing last month and the opposite a month or so later, all facts of course. As a result of exposing the fake news for what it is OANN is now under attack from them. The attacks are only on their own fake news media outlet, not in court. They can't take OANN to court because telling the truth is not a crime.

Fox Cable news: There is a lot more opinion here but they do give you straight news as well. Tucker Carlson, Sean Hannity and Laura Ingram (5:00, 6:00 and 7:00 pacific time respectively) are top notch. Hannity is number one as far as ratings go. He alone gets nearly the same amount of viewers as MSNBC and CNN combined during the same time period. Tucker Carson however is making a huge surge in ratings in his time slot and his ratings were already huge. People are waking up! On this station you will hear things not said on the Globalist controlled news. This part of Fox was not bought by Disney. This station as well as OANN have interviews with President Trump not even mentioned on the fake news. President Trump has recently come out against the management of Fox for the hiring of Donna Bazile who gave the questions in advance to Hillary in one of the presidential debates. I don't blame him for that and cannot understand Fox management's reasoning on that subject.

Judicial Watch: Tom Fitton is an attorney and its president. He is constantly using The Freedom of Information Act to hold our government accountable. It is because of his organization that as of March, 2020, Hillary will in the near future be deposed to answer for Benghazi and her use of private non secure emails. You can access Judicial Watch at Judicial Watch.org. I get updates daily on my phone.

BPR Daily: I get this daily on my phone as well. You can access BPR Daily at news@bizpacreview.com. Straight news, great source. They will typically give you ten or so news stories a day you will never hear on the Globalist controlled news.

The 700 Club: The first ten or fifteen minutes are world news that again, you will not hear on the controlled media.

The Epoch Times: Nonpartisan straight news. They've been around for about 20 years. They advertise their site something like this, 90 percent of the news you are exposed to comes from 6 corporations. They are right. They have undercover Chinese citizens giving them news on COVID-19… no easy task.

Project Veritas: This source is great at catching politicians and their under-lings on film discussing their underhanded and more often than not illegal plans.

American Thinker: If you like this book you will love their stuff…they have better writers.

Epilog

When one has a conversation about politics and especially President Trump, said person is on dangerous ground. The Globalist controlled media has done their job exceedingly well. I have heard friendships of decades go down the tubes on various social media platforms over this subject. There is a great deal of passion and misinformation out there. The misinformation is constant and like repetition it is the mother of learning. I have an attorney friend that does not like President Trump. As an attorney he knows how to argue a point. This is a man who's intelligence I have a great deal of respect for, yes, there are a few smart attorneys out there. After trying many tactics I believe I hit upon one that gave him pause for thought. I simply asked him had he ever heard of the CFR. His answer was no. I then gave him a quick synopsis of the history, founders and some of their handiwork. Though I did not bring him to the light then and there, I believe I planted a strong seed. The most important thing we must keep in mind when talking to President Trump haters is that we are dealing with a victim. A victim of a conspiracy that is over 100 years old. A victim who is drinking the Globalist cool aid and doesn't even know it. A conspiracy that has power and money at its disposal that we cannot fathom. We need to show compassion and a great, great deal of patience. One tactic that will never work is going down party lines. Trying to make a Democrat into a Republican or vice versa is disaster. Instead I try to unite with a common enemy in mind, the Globalists. I remind whomever I'm speaking to that in my entire adult life a never once voted for a Republican or a Democratic presidential candidate, until I voted for Presidential Candidate Donald Trump. Another tactic that I found useful before Coronavirus was to ask them how their 401K is doing.

In President Trump we have for the first time in decades a president who does not kowtow to Globalists. A president who puts America first. A president who is getting us out of senseless never ending wars. We have policed the world since the end of WW2. We did this on our dime. President Trump did not try to destabilize NATO as the fake news stated. He simply said hey; pay your fair share. The question is why didn't presidents for the last 70 years do the same? I sincerely hope this book shed light on the why. As of this writing President Trump has appointed over 192 Federal Judges. The fake news, true to form, said he appointed conservative judges. This is simply more rhetoric from the left. The true description of the judges he appointed is constitutional judges. Women and men who adjudicate based on the best document ever conceived for governance by mankind, the United States Constitution. If you like freedom of speech, the right to assemble, protection from unreasonable search and seizure etc. you should be happy with President Trumps Federal Judge appointees. For too long we've had judges legislating from the bench (especially the ninth circuit). That is not their job. This is why the founders split our government into three branches, the Executive, the Legislative and the Judicial. President Trump was fond of saying that the people that made our trade deals with China and other countries were bad deal makers. He was being nice. The trade deals were so woefully one sided on every other countries behalf save our own, that the people that made the deals were either the dumbest people that walked the earth, or had a completely different agenda in mind.

I will make you a promise. If President Trump wins the election, I promise the Globalist controlled media will continues its barrage of lies and innuendo backed by unnamed sources to paint him as some sort of Mephistopheles. These lies will continue for the next 4 years. These Democrats not in the know, not part of the CFR, will do as they are told by Democrats that are in the know to keep their elected posts. These lesser Democrats know the key to staying in power is to get along you must go along. The lesser Democrats know the power of the Democratic National Committee and how important money is for reelection. They also know that a President from another party that is truly making this country prosperous and safe is not good for their reelection bid, especially given the chaos in democratic run cities, Chicago (Chiraq as the locals call it), Baltimore, Seattle, Portland, Los Angeles, and of course New York City. There is another reason these lies will continue about President Trump; the last thing the Globalists want after 8 years of President Trump is another America first president, Mike Pence.

I hope that this book shed some light on our history and our present. I hope if you deem it worthy you will share it with others.